*The Investor's
Self-Teaching Seminars*

INVESTING IN MONEY MARKET SECURITIES

*One of a Series of Hands-On Workshops
Dedicated to the Serious Investor*

Jeffrey H. Katz

PROBUS PUBLISHING COMPANY
Chicago, Illinois

© 1991, Jeffrey H. Katz

ALL RIGHTS RESERVED. No part of this publication may be reproduced, stored in a retrieval system, or transmitted by any means, electronic, mechanical, photocopying, recording or otherwise, without the prior written permission of the publisher and the copyright holder.

This publication is designed to provide accurate and authoritative information in regard to the subject matter covered. It is sold with the understanding that the publisher is not engaged in rendering legal, accounting or other professional service.

Library of Congress Cataloging-in-Publication Data Available

ISBN 1-55738-147-X

Printed in the United States of America

BB

1 2 3 4 5 6 7 8 9 0

CONTENTS

PREFACE — v

CHAPTER ONE: INVESTING IN MONEY MARKET SECURITIES — 1

CHAPTER TWO: UNITED STATES TREASURY BILLS — 23

CHAPTER THREE: UNITED STATES GOVERNMENT AGENCY DISCOUNT NOTES — 41

CHAPTER FOUR: TIME DEPOSITS OF FINANCIAL INSTITUTIONS — 59

CHAPTER FIVE: BANKERS' ACCEPTANCES — 79

CHAPTER SIX: COMMERCIAL PAPER — 91

CHAPTER SEVEN: REPURCHASE AGREEMENTS	105
CHAPTER EIGHT: CASE STUDY	115
APPENDIX A: EXAMPLE ANSWERS	123
APPENDIX B: SUMMARY	147
APPENDIX C: CHARACTERISTICS CROSS REFERENCE	157
APPENDIX D: CHARACTERISTICS CROSS REFERENCE MATRICES	165
APPENDIX E: TAX EFFECTS	183
APPENDIX F: GLOSSARY	187
APPENDIX G: BIBLIOGRAPHY	199
ABOUT THE AUTHOR	203

PREFACE

All of us dream of the day when we will have enough money to purchase our "dream" house, "dream" car, trip abroad, or extensive wardrobe. We go to college, vocational school, medical school, or law school to learn a skill which we can use to earn the means to achieve these lifelong ambitions. Most of us however, never learn about all the financial products available which, when used properly, can help our funds grow so that we may achieve our objectives more quickly.

I have been employed in fixed-income securities sales for over eleven years. I have found that many individual investors are not knowledgeable about all of the securities available to them. Surprisingly, a number of individuals who are entrusted with investing for companies are not very knowledgeable either. The majority of those who invest for small- and medium-sized companies have many responsibilities other than investing. In many cases, they just do not have the time to learn everything there is to know about the products available. Therefore they may not be maximizing the return of their company's investable funds.

There is a wide range of financial products available, including stocks, bonds, options, real estate, and mutual funds. This Self-Teaching Seminar will explore short-term, fixed-income, debt securities, which are referred to as money market securities. These debt instruments mature in one year or less, and on the day of purchasing one of these securities, the investor knows exactly how much will be earned at maturity.

Most investors need to place at least a part of their portfolio in money market securities for several reasons. First, most investors want a portion of their funds maturing in under one year due to their cash flow needs, their purchases, or possible interest rate changes. Investors also want at least a portion of their portfolio in securities that have a known interest payment amount and interest payment date. This, of course helps in planning the payment of expenses. Furthermore, the securities in this book offer minimum denominations that are small enough for the individual or corporate investor. The reader will find these securities to be less risky than most other investment opportunities available. This is due to the credit worthiness of the issuers, the high degree of liquidity, and the short-term maturity. The low degree of risk is further enhanced because the investors of these securities rank high among those who will receive funds in the event of the issuer's bankruptcy. Investors have focused more on safety and liquidity of late, due to the recent stock market crashes. Hence, short-term debt securities have become even more popular. As individuals and companies earn more and the economy continues to grow, these securities (along with other financial products) will only increase in popularity and importance.

This seminar will discuss the securities that I have found to be the most popular among short-term investors: U.S. Treasury Bills, U.S. Government Agency Discount Notes, Bank Negotiable Certificates of Deposit, Bank Euro Certificates of Deposit, Bank Euro Time Deposits, Bankers Acceptances, Commercial Paper, and Repurchase Agreements.

Chapter One will present an overall discussion about money market securities and will discuss the questions each investor should answer before even considering which security to purchase.

Chapters Two through Seven will delve into each money market security. The topics under discussion will be definitions; purpose; safety; denominations; maturities; liquidity; taxation of earned income; form of interest payment; form of ownership; method of transaction; rate determination; characteristics appealing to investors; and formulas used to determine cost, interest earned, and yield to maturity. The reader will be asked to perform these calculations for the examples given.

Chapter Eight will test the reader on the knowledge gained in the previous chapters. Two case studies will be presented where the reader will be asked to make decisions based on an investors' needs, goals, and constraints.

The appendices will provide the reader with a summary of the facts from Chapters Two through Seven for quick reference. The summary will be in the form of bullet points on each security, cross reference lists, and matrices. After reading this Self-Teaching Seminar, you should be knowledgeable enough to consider including these securities in your investment portfolio. At the very least, you should be better prepared to converse with investment brokers, counselors, and order-takers who will execute your investment decisions.

Chapter One

INVESTING IN MONEY MARKET SECURITIES

Money market securities, also referred to as short-term debt securities, are those securities that mature in one year or less from the date of issuance. The securities discussed in this book are also commonly known as fixed-income securities. With fixed-income securities, the investor knows on the day of purchase the maturity date and exactly how much interest will be earned at maturity. Still another name for the securities in this book is cash equivalents. This refers to the fact that the securities mature in a relatively short period of time and are easily convertible into cash should the need arise before maturity.

The securities under discussion here will include the short-term debt obligations of the federal government (Treasury Bills), U.S. government agencies (discount notes of the Federal Farm Credit Banks, Federal Home Loan Banks, Federal National Mortgage Association and Federal Home Loan Mortgage Corp.), banks (certificates of deposit, Euro certificates of deposit, Bankers' Acceptances, and Euro time deposits), and corporations (commercial paper). Repurchase agreements also will be discussed.

Money market securities are issued when one of the institutions mentioned above needs funds for operations, expansion, or any number of reasons. The debt is the promise that after a stated period of time the debt-issuing entity will pay back its creditors (investors for the purposes of this text) their originally invested funds, (principal), plus a stated return (interest). The interest will be "simple interest" which is interest earned on the principal only. This is different from "compound interest" which is interest earned on both the principal and any previously earned interest.

The securities under discussion in this book are among the most popular investment vehicles today. There are several reasons for this phenomenon. Most investors wish to have at least a portion of their investment portfolio in securities where it is known exactly how much will be earned and on what date. This just seems to make sense. With this knowledge, the investor can better plan his cash flow. Also, most investors like to have at least a portion of their investment portfolio maturing in under one year. Investors have a certain sense of security knowing that part of their portfolio will mature in the near future. This gives them the opportunity to reevaluate their financial needs, expectations of interest rate movements and other economic opportunities. Furthermore, the high degree of liquidity offered by these securities, gives the investor the comfort of knowing that should an unforeseen emergency arise, he has quick access to cash. The investment community considers the securities discussed in this book to be among the safest securities available today.

Most professional investment managers will tell you that a diversified portfolio is the best means of establishing good long-term performance. A diversified portfolio is a group of investments that has been divided among different types of securities and issuers. This method of structuring an investment portfolio is used as a way of reducing the risk of the total portfolio. Therefore, for many investors, investing all available money in short-term, fixed-income securities at all times may not be the best strategy. For example, there are other investments, such as stocks and real estate, that historically have been better long-term hedges against inflation. But, placing at least a portion of one's portfolio in short-term, fixed-income, relatively safe, relatively liquid instruments makes sense for investors whose goal is diversification and safety.

The percentage of one's portfolio that should be made up of these securities will be different for every investor. An investor's portfolio mix at any one time is determined by a number of factors: aversion to risk, expectation of interest rate movement, financial goals, personal goals, amount of investable funds, tax considerations, and the current and expected economic situation.

The investor must realize one of the most basic principals in finance before determining his portfolio mix: there is a direct correlation between the amount of return an investor can expect to receive and the amount of risk incurred. Thus, the higher the risk an investor is willing to assume, the higher the potential rewards. The securities under discussion in this text are considered to be less risky than most investments offered today. The upside potential for these securities is limited to the rate of return stated at the time of purchase.

There are other investments, such as stocks, where the investor does not know how much will be earned. The purchaser of stock buys an ownership share in a company. If the company does poorly or goes bankrupt, the investor may lose all or part of the investment. This is the high risk incurred by owners of stocks. On the other hand, should the company perform well, the stockholders' rewards theoretically are unlimited.

All this talk about the relative low risk of the short-term securities under discussion here does not mean that they are riskless. On the contrary, there are several inherent risks and costs of investing in these securities: default risk, liquidity risk, inflation risk, principal risk, and opportunity cost.

Default risk is the chance that the issuer will not pay back to the investor all or part of the original principal or the interest owed or both. The institutions backing the securities in this text are the U.S. government, U.S. government agencies, commercial banks, and corporations. There is virtually no default risk with securities backed by the U.S. government because of the government's ability to tax the public. U.S. government agency securities are considered relatively safe because, although not a direct obligation, they are considered a moral obligation of the U.S. government. The U.S. government also guarantees bank deposits up to $100,000. In the investment community, there is nothing safer than a security backed by the U.S. government.

All of the other securities in this book are backed by the creditworthiness of the issuing institution. Investors will find that the securities in this book that are not backed by the U.S. government are backed by large, well-known, highly reputable corporations or banks. To further help potential investors become acquainted with institutions issuing debt, financial data and credit ratings of banks and corporations are readily available. Moody's, and Standard and Poor's are two examples of rating agencies whose purpose is to help investors determine the creditworthiness of institutions. Through their analysis, they establish a rating, which is an opinion of the institution's ability to pay back principal and interest. Based on these ratings, the investor can decide whether or not he is comfortable buying securities issued by the institution.

The institutions discussed in this book are either considered riskless or are backed by large, highly reputable entities that are highly scrutinized. Furthermore, holders of money market securities are among the first paid off in the event of bankruptcy. However, the investor should be aware that in lending money there is always the risk of default.

Liquidity risk is the ability of the investor to obtain invested funds back instantly before a security matures. This, of course, becomes important to the investor in the event of an unforeseen expense or the desire to invest in a superior investment opportunity. Money market securities are considered highly liquid compared to alternative investments. However, these securities differ among themselves as to their relative degree of liquidity.

The factor that determines the degree of liquidity of a security is the breadth of its secondary market. The secondary market is the market where previously issued securities are bought and sold. Thus, these securities are referred to as secondary securities (secondary, CDs, Euro CDs, etc.). U.S. Treasury Bills, with their large, active, organized secondary market, offer investors a high degree of liquidity. The other securities in this book offer the investor a lesser degree of liquidity because their secondary markets are not as large or efficient. To discourage investors from cashing in their securities before maturity, some issuers penalize the investor for early withdrawal. So there are various degrees of liquidity among money market securities. Everything else being equal, the security with a lesser degree of liquidity will offer the investor a higher return as compensation.

Inflation risk is the risk that the general level of prices will rise during the time the investor holds a security thereby "eating away" its "real" return. For example, let's say an investor purchases a security with an 8 percent annual rate of return when inflation is a 3 percent annual rate. The investor has a 5 percent "real" return over inflation. If inflation rises over the life of the security, to say 4 percent, the investor's real return now diminishes to 4 percent. Of course, the flip side to this scenario is that if the rate of inflation decreases over the life of the security the investor's real return increases.

Principal risk is typically of greater concern to investors of longer term securities. However, should an investor purchase a money market security and then have to liquidate before maturity, principal risk could be a concern. Although a money market security carries a stated rate of interest, market rates continue to fluctuate during the security's life. There is an inverse relationship between a security's price and its yield. For example, if interest rates rise after purchase, the price of the security, with its stated return, will fall. Therefore, the investor who must sell prior to maturity will receive an amount that is less than the principal originally invested. This occurs because prospective buyers of the security can now purchase similar newly issued securities (primary securities) at a higher return, due to the general rise in interest rates. Potential buyers will consider purchasing the lower-yielding security only at a reduced price, which directly affects the amount of principal received by the seller (the original investor). Of course, if interest rates fall, the price of the security will rise because its return is higher relative to newly issued securities.

Opportunity cost is simply what the investor gives up by not investing in some other instrument. There is a vast array of financial products available today and each product has a particular degree of liquidity risk, safety risk, and so forth, and a particular return. Each investor decides which security to purchase based on their own set of priorities. With any security in this book, as with anything that we spend our money on, there is a certain opportunity cost to not purchasing an alternative. For example, an investor may decide to purchase a Treasury Bill maturing in one year at 8 percent. His decision is based on his set of priorities which make the Treasury Bill attractive. At the same time, this investor could have purchased another security maturing in one year yielding 10 percent. Obviously this 10 percent-yielding security had certain characteristics that did not appeal to the investor. For example, the security might be backed by an institution that the investor does not feel comfortable lending to. For this reason and others, the investor decides to pass up a security offering a higher return and purchases the lower-yielding security. In this case, the opportunity cost is the difference in yield between the two alternatives, or the 2 percent, which is forgone by opting for the lower yielding security.

The above example is a perfect segue into the next section of this chapter: a security's rate of return is not the only thing for an investor to consider before making the purchase decision. The investor must first consider his financial and personal needs, priorities, and restrictions before even thinking about rate of return. The investor should answer the following questions before going on to the next step which is shopping for the security:

1. How much do I have in investable funds?
2. What are my cash flow needs?
3. How liquid must my investment be?
4. What is my aversion to risk?
5. What is my tax situation?
6. How do I want my interest paid?
7. How do I expect interest rates to move in the future?

Obviously the first question any potential investor must ask is, "Do I have any money to invest, and if so, how much?" In some cases, the investor's investable funds may be less than the minimum amount required by an issuer, and thus the potential investor cannot invest. Typically, the smallest face amount available is $1,000 or $5,000.

The "investment urge" typically will develop when the investor finds his savings accumulating in a checking account, savings account, money market account, or mutual fund. The holder of the account, upon seeing these funds accumulate to a point felt to be substantial, may ask, "Since I know I will not need these funds for 'X' period of time, is there a secure investment where I can earn a decent rate of return?" Although there are many investments available today, with various minimum amounts, the potential investor should realize that an amount of even $5,000 will only gain him access to a few of the securities in this book. The investor really needs to have accumulated much more to have the opportunity to choose from all of them. The specific minimum amounts needed for each security will be discussed in the following chapters.

So, the investor knows that he has enough funds to invest in at least one of the securities under discussion. Now he must consider cash flow needs; he must answer the question, "Do I need these funds for the payment of some future expense?" In some cases, the investor simply does not expect to need these funds for any future expense. Then the investor can use these "excess" funds to produce a portfolio mix that maximizes his total return based on his aversion to risk, expectations of interest rate movements, expectations of economic developments, and so forth.

In other cases, the investor is aware that these "excess" funds will be required for the payment of an expense on some future date. Whether it is a company or an individual, there may be a higher priority use for these funds in the future. The company may need these invested funds for the payment of a major expense, expansion, salaries, taxes; the list is endless. Likewise, the individual may need the funds for the purchase of a home or car, payment of taxes, college education, and so on. The key point here is that the investor's priorities may change. Today, and for "X" days, these funds are not needed for any particular use; the holder of the funds wants to earn interest instead of just letting them idle. Then "X" days from today, these funds will be called upon for a higher priority use. It is essential at this point that the investor try to determine what that higher priority might be and when it might occur. The investor then can place the money in a security that matures on or before the date that the funds will needed for another purpose.

Consider the following example. Paula has $10,000 in excess funds. She has learned from her accountant that she owes the state and federal governments $10,000 in taxes, due April 15 which is three months from today. With no other use for these funds until April 15, Paula can invest in a security to mature on or before April 15. The payment of her taxes on April 15 is the higher priority use for the $10,000 on that date. Paula does not care if she can earn a higher return on her funds if she invests in a security maturing after April 15: the payment of her taxes with this money takes priority on that date.

Now the investor knows how much is available for investment and when these funds are needed. He asks, "What happens if for some unforeseen reason I need my funds back before the security is due to mature?" This is referred to as the "liquidity need." From the time the investor purchases the security until the time it matures, any of the following may occur: an emergency or forgotten expense, or a superior alternate investment opportunity. When any of these occur, the investor may have to liquidate, or convert into cash, the security. Once again, the priority use of these funds has suddenly shifted.

Money market securities vary in their ease of conversion into cash. The investor must realize that everything else equal, the more liquid a security is, the less its return to the investor. And, of course, the less liquid, the more return. Once this rule is understood, it is up to the investor to determine how important the liquidity of a security is. Some investors may feel confident that they will not have to liquidate their investment before maturity, and may be willing to invest in a security that is less liquid but offers a higher return. In other cases, investors either are not sure if they will have to liquidate their investment before maturity or simply feel more comfortable owning a security that has a higher degree of liquidity. This type of investor might purchase a U.S. Treasury Bill, which is highly liquid but may offer a lower yield. This relates to that simple financial concept: the investor is rewarded for incurring more risk.

Securities differ in their liquidity because the breadth of their secondary markets differ. Typically when an investor converts his security into cash, he is selling the security to a financial institution and receiving the cash proceeds. Often these proceeds will include not only the going price for that security at the time of sale, but also interest that has accrued on the security up to that point in time. Upon buying the security from an investor, the financial institution may turn around and sell this security to another investor or financial institution, preferably at a profit. U.S. Treasury Bills are considered the most liquid money market security because they offer the largest, most efficient secondary market in the world. This statement means that once the financial institution purchases a U.S. Treasury Bill, it can easily turn around and find a purchaser for the security. In fact, one of the most important tasks of primary dealers in U.S. government securities is to create a market (establish a price at which they would buy or sell a U.S. Treasury security) at all times. This insures investors of liquidity. Furthermore, there are more outstanding U.S. Treasury securities and potential buyers of them than any other security under discussion in this text. Euro CDs, on the other hand, although convertible into cash, do not offer the investor the same degree of liquidity as a Treasury issue. There simply are not as many Euro CD securities outstanding or Euro CD buyers to provide a secondary market as broad as that for Treasury securities. This is just one of the reasons that investors will find Euro CDs offering a higher yield than comparable maturing U.S. Treasury Bills. It is the investor who must determine how important liquidity is relative to return.

The next question an investor must ask is one of the most important: "How safe do I feel investing my funds in a security backed by a certain issuer?" Once again, there is a direct correlation between risk and return. The higher the perceived risk that the guarantor of the security will not pay back invested funds, the higher the return to the investor (everything else equal).

The chances that the guarantor might run into financial difficulties and thus not be able to pay back the investor's principal and interest are greater the longer the investor holds the security. Hence, under normal circumstances an investor receives a higher return for the same security if held longer. This scenario, however, does not always exist in the marketplace. There are times when a longer maturing security will offer a lower return than an otherwise identical security with a shorter maturity. This may occur, for example, when interest rates are widely expected to fall. Typically, at least in theory, investors need to be enticed with a higher return to keep their funds invested longer with any issuer.

The investment community considers the securities discussed in this book to be among the safest available. The extreme degree of safety associated with securities backed explicitly or implicitly by the U.S. government has already been discussed. Now we will consider securities issued by banks and corporations. The banks and corporations that issue money market securities are a diverse group. They are based in different regions, are of different sizes, have different financial conditions, have different business focuses, and so forth. In essence, each entity has its own perceived risk in the eyes of investors, based on these conditions. Only the investor can define his comfort level in lending to any one issuer, based on the issuer's name and reputation or through studying the issuer's financial statements, history, business focus, and credit ratings. The investor's ultimate decision depends on both his perception of the issuer and his aversion to risk.

What follows is an elementary example of "aversion to risk." Diane and Steve each have $100,000 to invest for six months. Today, U.S. Treasury Bills are yielding 8 percent, while General Motors commercial paper is yielding 8.50 percent. Both know that they will not need their $100,000 during this six-month period. Diane considers herself very conservative. Although she has heard of General Motors, she feels more comfortable investing in a government-backed security. Therefore, although the GM commercial paper offers a higher yield, she opts for the T-Bill. Steve, on the other hand, not only feels comfortable investing in such a big, well known corporation for six months, but feels it is silly to pass up the higher return. Thus, he invests in the GM commercial paper. Each investor purchased the security that felt most comfortable. Both choices were correct considering each investor's aversions to risk.

A question that is always on the mind of investors is, "How is the income I receive from my investments taxed?" Investors should be concerned not only with the rate of return, but also with how much money they will earn after taxes. All the securities in this book are taxed by the federal government. Some securities are also taxed by the investor's state government, while others are state-tax-free.

Always consult your accountant when you have questions concerning how your particular tax situation could affect your investment decision. Often an investor's tax situation determines if it is more advantageous to invest in a state-tax-free security. Furthermore, states differ in the way they treat the investment income earned by individuals and corporations.

When an investor receives a rate quote on a security, he is typically obtaining a quote before any taxes are considered. The total return ultimately received by the investor will be less than the quoted rate because the federal government takes a percentage of the interest earned and, in some cases, the state does also.

The following example demonstrates the importance of one's tax situation in deciding between investment alternatives. KJB Studios has $100,000 to invest for one year. Their particular needs and restrictions have dictated that they are indifferent between investing in their local bank's certificate of deposit or a U.S. Treasury Bill. The deciding factor will be which of these two alternatives produces the higher net return. Income received from CDs is taxed by the investor's state while income from T-Bills is not. KJB has been quoted a 10 percent yield on the CD, while a similar maturing T-Bill offers a 9.50 percent yield (both are quoted on a CD equivalent yield basis, which we will learn more about later). The state that KJB is located in taxes corporations on the income they receive from state-taxable investments, at a rate of 10 percent. We will assume for this example that the federal government taxes KJB at a rate of 15 percent on investment income.

At first glance it appears that KJB should invest in the CD. After all, KJB is indifferent between the CD and the T-Bill, yet the CD is being offered at a higher rate of return. Upon a closer look however, we may find a different answer. With the CD, KJB will earn a gross income of $10,000 for one year ($100,000 investment multiplied by 10 percent). We will assume that buying a $100,000 T-Bill for one year at a CD equivalent yield of 9.50 percent will produce gross earnings of $9,000 (We will learn how to calculate the income

Exhibit 1

	CD Yielding 10% for One Year	T-Bill Yielding 9.50% for One Year
Income:	$10,000	$9,000
Fed Tax (15%)	–$1,500	–$1,350
State Tax (10%)	–$1,000	–$0
Total Net Income:	$7,500	$7,650

on T-Bills in Chapter 2). This problem is broken down mathematically in Exhibit 1.

In this case, KJB is better off investing in the T-Bill which will earn $150 more, net of taxes. This does not mean that a state-tax-free security will produce more net income then a state-taxable security every time for every investor. Please understand your own income tax bracket and how the state you reside in treats income on investments. This can definitely affect your investment decision.

Choosing the type of interest payment the investor will receive is usually of less importance relative to the issues already discussed. One method by which interest is paid is referred to as "interest-bearing," or "interest at maturity." In this case, the interest on the security is paid at maturity (or semiannually if the security matures in one year or more) at a stated percentage of the principal originally invested. For example, let's say an investor purchases a security for $100,000. This security matures one year from the date of issuance and has a stated coupon rate of return of 8 percent. Therefore, one year from this purchase, the investor will receive from the issuing entity his $100,000 original investment, or principal, plus $8,000 in interest ($100,000 multiplied by 8 percent).

The other method by which interest on money market securities is paid is called "discounted." When a security is purchased on a discount basis, the investor pays an amount less than the security's face value and receives the face amount at maturity. For example, let's say an investor purchases a $10,000 discounted security. On the date of purchase, less than the $10,000 is actually invested, say $9,750. At maturity, $10,000 will be received back, thus earning in interest the difference between what was originally paid, $9,750, and what was received at maturity, $10,000, or $250.

Typically an investor's major needs and restrictions will lead to an investment decision. How interest is paid is typically not a major factor in the decision making process. There are securities, such as CDs and commercial paper, that offer an investor the choice of purchasing it at a discount or on an interest-bearing basis. There are investors who may not wish to purchase a discounted security because they may have available, and wish to have invested, the entire face amount. Once again, it really comes down to the investor's preference.

The expectations of future interest rate movements also should be considered before making the investment decision. The reader must realize that often even the "experts" are befuddled in their efforts to determine where interest rates are heading. There are well-paid economists, traders, portfolio managers, corporate treasurers, and other forecasters who try to predict the direction of interest rates over a particular time horizon. Even these "experts" are not always right in their assessment. Among the factors which may, individually or in concert, affect the movement of interest rates, are inflation, economic growth, monetary growth, political developments, and balance of payments.

There may be times when an investor cannot consider where interest rates may go, when making the investment decision. For example, an investor may need his funds back in a week for the payment of an expense. Sure, he may feel that interest rates will be heading down and wish to "lock in" his investment for longer, but the fact that he needs these funds in a week is a restriction.

There are investors who simply do not have an opinion on the future movement of interest rates. These investors, and others, may seek out the advice of "experts" or the media to conjure up an opinion on the direction of rates. Some investors may simply not consider the future movement of rates when making their decision.

Considering interest rate expectations in the investment decision can prove advantageous to the investor if the assessment turns out to be correct. Very simply, if an investor feels interest rates will decline over the investment horizon, he should lock in the current rate of return by investing in the longest maturity possible. If this assessment is correct, the investor will have earned a higher return than the current yields offered during the life of the investment. Conversely, if an investor feels that interest rates will rise, he should keep the maturity of his investment short and reinvest his funds during the investment period. If the assessment is correct, the investor will have maximized his return based on the time horizon and investment vehicle used.

To review, the investor at this point knows how much money is available for investment, how long a maturity is desired, what institution(s) the investor feels most secure lending to, how important liquidity is, how the investor's particular tax situation will affect the investment earnings, and whether the security should be purchased in a discounted or interest-bearing form. The investor may also have an opinion about where interest rates are headed. Based on these factors, the investor can determine which securities meet his criteria. The next step is to obtain rate quotes from a financial institution, broker, or other selling institution for the maturity range desirable for these securities. The investor can use these rate quotes to decide which security offers the highest return within the established parameters.

When shopping for a security, the investor receives an offer price quote, often just called an "offer," from the institution that is chosen for the transaction. This offer represents the price at which the institution is willing to sell the security to the investor. When selling a security, the investor receives a "bid" price quote, which represents the price at which the institution is willing to purchase the security.

Whether buying or selling a security, the investor should receive two types of rate quotes. One reflects the cost and stated earnings, and the other reflects the investor's total yield on an annual basis.

Whether a person purchases a car, house, or security, the cost is always considered. This establishes if sufficient funds are available for the purchase and serves as a means of comparison between alternatives. Because there are two possible ways to purchase a security, discounted or interest-bearing, there are also two ways of quoting the interest rate and cost. When the investor receives a quote on an interest-bearing instrument, it will be in the form of a coupon rate, say 7.50 percent, which is the percentage rate that the investor will earn on the principal. Obviously, the higher the quoted coupon rate the more the investor earns. When purchasing a primary, interest-bearing security, at the time of issuance the cost is always the invested principal. (Purchases of previously issued securities are slightly different, as will be discussed later in the book.)

The rate quoted on a discounted security, referred to as the discount rate, is the rate used to determine the difference between the purchase price and the face value. A higher discount rate translates into a higher discount off of the face amount of the investment, hence a lower price to the investor. When the purchase price is lower, the investor earns more relative to the initial outlay of funds. This discount rate will be quoted as a percentage, say 8.37 percent. The investor must then calculate his up-front cost based on this discount and the face value amount. (We will show you how in Chapter 2.)

The other rate quote received from your financial institution is commonly called its "yield to maturity." This rate, also quoted as a percentage, represents the average annual rate of return if the security is held to maturity. The yield to maturity provides the investor with a method of comparing a security's rate of return to that of other securities. Obviously the higher this yield, the better for the investor. There are many different types of yield to maturity quotes, each with its own formula. Two that are commonly used with money market securities are the money market (or CD equivalent) yield and the bond equivalent yield. The following chapters will describe how to determine the appropriate yield to maturity for each security. For now, simply be aware that when using yield to maturity to compare two or more securities you must quote the rates based on the same yield method for all of the securities in question. Otherwise you will be comparing "apples to oranges," and it will not be an accurate comparison.

Investors often ask how the yield and price of a security are determined. After all, did the institution quoting the rates just pull them out from thin air? There are several factors that affect the level of the rates on all securities in general. Furthermore, there are other factors that affect the yield on each particular security, which will be explored in the following chapters. First, the overall level of a security's yield is determined by the general level of interest rates for all investment products. For example, there were periods in the past when inflation was high, and to combat this the Federal Reserve tightened credit policy, thereby driving security yields into the 14 percent to 19 percent range. On the other hand, during periods of slow economic growth, the Federal Reserve has eased credit policy, bringing yields on securities well into the single digits. So, the overall economic and inflationary conditions influence the Federal Reserve to tighten or ease monetary policy, and this in turn will determine generally what securities will yield. Of course, because money market securities are among the safest securities available, they tend to be offered at among the lowest rates in the current marketplace.

Speculation regarding the general direction of interest rates can influence the yield of securities. The consensus among market participants regarding the direction of rates will produce an overall buying or selling trend in securities. The basic rule to consider is that if the overall market expects rates in the near future to fall, investors are more apt to buy securities to lock in their yield before rates fall. Consequently, there will be an increased demand for securities, today's placing added pressure for yields to fall further tomorrow. The flipside of this occurs when investors expect interest rates to rise. Investors are more apt to hold back their purchases in expectation of rates rising. The less demand for securities puts pressures on issuers to raise yields to attract investors.

There is a general market buy (bid) price and sell (offer) price for every security. For example, at a particular moment, T-Bills maturing in three months are generally selling for "X" price, top-rated U.S. bank CDs maturing in one month are generally selling for "Y percent" yield, and top-rated industrial commercial paper maturing in two months is generally selling for "Z percent" yield. Most transactions will take place at or near this market price. As a rule of thumb, the larger the size of the transaction, the better the terms of the investment, off of the general market price.

The price an investor pays for a security can also be influenced by the selling institution's interest rate expectations and strategy. From the investor's perspective, there are two key people within the selling institution, the trader and the sales person. The trader is the person who monitors the securities markets and sets the price at which the institution is willing to buy or sell a particular security. The trader communicates the price to the salesperson, who then presents it to the investor. The trader's goal is to sell securities at a higher price than he paid for the security. This is how traders generate profits. They are very sensitive to the movement of interest rates since an increase in rates while they own the security means a decrease in price (a loss to the trader). Remember, there is an inverse relation between a security's price and its yield. To avoid confusion, and because we are really talking about the same thing, when using examples to explain this section, only the price of the security will be considered. If the trader believes that prices of securities will rise soon he will want to hold onto the securities already owned and may try to purchase more to sell later at higher prices. This trader will be more willing to purchase securities and less willing to sell securities at the present time. If, on the other hand, the trader believes that prices of securities will fall soon, the trader will not want to own securities and will be much more willing to sell securities than to buy. Whatever the trader's bias, it will be directly reflected in the prices he gives to investors via the salesperson.

Let's use some actual prices to clarify all of this. We will first use an example of a trader who believes that prices of securities will rise soon. An investor wishes to purchase a security, whose selling price in the marketplace is currently 100. The trader may quote a price of say 101 because he does not want to sell the security and miss the opportunity to sell later at an even higher price. Only if the investor is willing to buy the securities at 101, which is higher than the current market price, will the trader part with the securities at this time. So you can see that the price quoted to the investor by this particular institution may not be as favorable as those from another institution due to this trader's expectations.

Now let's say the trader believes that the prices of securities will fall in the near future. We'll assume that the market price of the security that the investor wishes to purchase is still at 100. This time the trader quotes the investor a price of 99 because he is more eager to sell before prices drop. The investor receives a more favorable quote now from this same institution relative to the offer prices of other institutions.

Another factor that could influence the price quoted is the trader's ownership position in the particular security, the investor wants to purchase. If the trader already owns the security, he is likely to offer a relatively favorable price to the investor. If he does not, he will have to obtain it from another institution in order to sell it to you. Like any other profit business, the trader will have to mark up the security in order to cover the transaction costs and obtain a profit.

The supply of a security available to investors is the other side of the equation determining the price of a security. The economic maxim is, the smaller the supply of an item, the higher the price. Suppose demand for securities is high among investors because they expect prices to rise, and at the same time issuers are reducing the amount of money market securities being offered to investors. This will tend to put upward pressure on the price of these securities and reduce their yield. We will discuss in later chapters the factors that may influence issuers to alter the amount of their securities they sell to the public.

Typically, when an investor buys or sells a security, the dealer or institution sends a written confirmation statement of the transaction to the investor. On most confirmation statements, the purchase or sale price and yield to maturity are presented. Among the other information typically found on this statement are: the transaction date, date that funds are transferred from buyer to seller (settlement date), the institution's name and address, the investor's name and address, the security transacted, the issuer, the date the security was issued, the maturity date, the coupon (if applicable), the interest payment date(s), the investor's account number with the institution, and the method of payment. The following chapters will present the formulas, along with examples, for cost, interest earned and yield to maturity for each type of money market security to give the reader a better understanding of these figures.

The investor should be aware that there are several different types of settlement dates: cash settlement, regular settlement, skip settlement, and corporate settlement. Cash settlement means that funds and securities are exchanged the same day that the transaction is enacted. Regular settlement means that securities and funds will be exchanged on the next business day. Skip settlement occurs two business days after the date of the transaction. Corporate settlement occurs five business days after the date of transaction. Settlements longer than five business days are referred to as corporate-plus-one, corporate-plus-two, double-corporate, and so forth. Settlement occurs on the day agreed upon by both buyer and seller and is a function of the willingness and ability of both parties to pay for and deliver the securities.

Another piece of information on the confirmation statement that the investor may find is the form that the securities are held in. As proof of ownership, securities are held in one of three forms: book-entry, bearer, or registered. A security in book-entry form is actually held as a computer entry on the books of the institution chosen by the investor. The only actual proof of ownership for the investor is his transaction confirmation statement and account statement. Some of these book-entry securities may be wired from one institution to another, if the investor so chooses.

A security held in bearer form is actually a physical security, a negotiable certificate that states the terms of the instrument. This certificate does not have the name of the investor on it, and because the certificate is negotiable anyone can cash it in for the proceeds. Because of this risk, it is highly recommended that investors keep bearer certificates in a secure place. Most investors safekeep their bearer certificates with the institution they purchased them from. There are some securities which are physically held, and available for delivery, in only one city. All bankers' acceptances, for example, are only held and deliverable in New York City. Most large institutions have safekeeping custodians in New York in order to hold these and other securities.

A registered security is the same as a bearer security except that a registered certificate has the investor's name embossed on it, making it non-negotiable. Only the investor can cash in and receive the proceeds from the security. Registered securities are not a popular form among investors today. There is typically a cost involved in registering certificates. Most investors today prefer the ease and convenience of book-entry and bearer form. In fact, some securities are available only in book-entry or bearer form.

By now you understand how money market securities originate, why an investor should even consider them for his investment portfolio, what risks are associated with them, what the investor must consider before shopping for rate quotes, what rates will be quoted, how rates are determined in general, and what is on a confirmation statement. The following six chapters will take the reader through a more detailed discussion of the most popular money market securities.

*Chapter
Two*

UNITED STATES TREASURY BILLS

United States Treasury bills (also referred to as: Treasury Bills, T-Bills, or Bills) are the short-term, direct obligation of the United States federal government. This security is used by the federal government as an important tool in the management of the federal debt. Because the U.S. government currently spends more money than it receives in the form of taxes and fees, it must issue debt to make up the difference. Part of the debt that it issues is in the form of Treasury Bills.

The Federal Reserve Bank uses Treasury Bills as a tool in the execution of monetary policy. Monetary policy is the Federal Reserve Bank's management of the supply of credit and thus the level of interest rates. Among the many tools "the Fed" uses to influence interest rates is the buying and selling of large amounts of Treasury Bills.

U.S. Treasury Bills are among the most popular money market instruments purchased by investors today. Among the features which attract investors to Treasury Bills are their high degree of safety (low default risk), high degree of liquidity, favorable tax feature, and low minimum denomination. Another feature which investors find appealing is that Treasury Bills are purchased on a discount basis. This means that the investor pays less than the stated face value of the security at the time of purchase and receives the face value at maturity. For some investors, not having to come up with the entire face value at the time of the purchase can improve affordability.

Treasury Bills are considered the safest security available to investors today. The reason for this is quite simple: Treasury Bills are backed by the full faith and credit of the U.S. government. Securities with this guarantee are considered riskless by the investment community because of the U.S. government's history of no defaults and political stability, and its ability to tax the public.

Treasury bills are offered with a minimum face value of $10,000. Over $10,000, T-Bills can be purchased in increments of $5,000. For example, investors may purchase T-Bills in face amounts of $15,000, $20,000, $135,000, and so forth. Remember, investors actually pay an amount less than this face value and receive the face value at maturity.

T-Bills are usually issued with maturities of three months, six months, or one year. The longest maturity available for a bill is one year. Every Monday, the Treasury issues new three- and six-month maturing bills. New one-year bills are usually issued on the last Thursday of every month. These newly issued bills are referred to as "current issues." Investors may also purchase bills that don't mature in exactly three months, six months, or one year. These bills are referred to as either "non-current" or "outstanding" bills. Outstanding bills are those that were issued in a prior week. All bills mature on Thursday of the week they are due.

The Treasury issues bills through an auction method. The price of newly issued bills is determined through the competitive bidding of investors at the Treasury's auction. When buying bills at the auction, most investors place a "noncompetitive" order with their institution or local Federal Reserve Bank, which means they pay the average auction price determined by "competitive" bids. A noncompetitive order includes the following information: the face amount desired for purchase, the specific bill desired for purchase, and the institution that will safekeep the bills for the investor. Competitive bids typically are placed by large investors such as dealers, banks, insurance companies, money funds, and foreign central banks. These investors will send to the Treasury their bid, i.e., what price they are willing to pay for a specific amount of a specific new bill. These large investors watch the movement of the bill market very closely and try to obtain their bills at a price below the auction average. Thus their goal is to bid a price that will assure that they will obtain the bills they want but is less than the average of all competitive bids received by the Treasury. These competitive bidders will not necessarily receive any or all their desired bills. Once all the bids are in, the Treasury distributes bills to the highest bidders until it has distributed the entire issue. The Treasury announces later that same day (typically around 4:00PM Eastern standard time) the average auction price, which is the price noncompetitive investors will pay for their bills. At this time also, the competitive bidders will learn how many bills they received. Once placing a noncompetitive bid, the investor is committed to whatever price is set by the auction. Payment for newly issued bills is always made on the Thursday following the auction.

Investors purchase "non-current" bills from a financial institution at whatever price the institution is willing to sell to them. This kind of purchase is referred to as buying the bills in the secondary market. Whether buying or selling a bill, the investor tells the institution's salesperson the face amount of the security to be transacted, the maturity date of the bill, and the institution that will safekeep the bills for the investor. At this time, the salesperson tells the investor the discount rate (price) at which the institution will buy or sell the bills. If this price is acceptable to the investor, the transaction is completed. Settlement for non-current bills typically occurs the next business day (regular settlement), but may take place as early as the same day of the transaction (cash settlement). On settlement date, whether the bills are bought at the auction or in the secondary market, the proceeds for the purchase usually is debited from an account designated by the investor. Typically at maturity this same account is credited with the face value of the bills. Should the investor sell before maturity, this account will be credited with the proceeds of the sale.

There are two other types of bills that the investor should also be aware of. The first type is called a "When-Issued" bill. All bills become "When-Issued," or "W.I.," as soon as the Treasury announces the date of the bill's auction, usually one week before the auction. Investors can purchase these bills through their financial institution at their prevailing market price. These W.I. bills essentially are traded in the market before they are issued. W.I. bills are popular among investors who trade bills for speculation. These speculators purchase W.I. bills with the hope that the price will appreciate so they can sell them at a profit. W.I. bills are appealing to speculators because they do not have to pay for their purchases until the bills settle, about one week following the auction. In fact, if a speculator sells the bills before the settlement date, he does not have to pay for the purchase at all; the investor receives only his profit from (or pays his loss to) the financial institution that executed the trades.

The other bill the investor should be aware of is called the "Cash Management bill." This type of bill is usually issued by the Treasury to get them through temporary cash flow shortages. These issues are infrequently announced by the Treasury and typically have short maturities. The announcement of an issue includes settlement and maturity dates and the size of the issue. As with other bills, the issue price is determined by the competitive bids at their auction.

All bills are bought and sold in book-entry form (held as a computer entry at the investor's financial institution). The confirmation and account statements are the investor's physical proof of ownership. Bills may be wired from one financial institution to another. An investor may purchase the bill from one institution, yet want another institution to maintain the record of ownership. When this occurs, the investor simply instructs the selling institution to wire the bills to the other institution. Most investors choose one institution that maintains their records and safekeeps their securities, although investors may buy from and sell to any institution.

A very appealing quality of bills is their high degree of liquidity. They are more liquid than any of the other securities in this book. Bills are highly liquid because they are bought and sold in a large, organized, and efficient secondary market. There are more buyers and sellers of bills than of any other money market security. The existence of the primary dealers in government securities helps ensure the liquidity of these issues for investors. At all times, these primary dealers must be willing and able to bid a price to buy a bill from an investor needing to sell.

Investors also enjoy a tax benefit by investing in bills. The interest earned on bills is taxed by the federal government but not by state governments. This can be the deciding factor when choosing between alternative investments. A bill may actually net the investor a higher return than an alternative with a higher stated interest rate whose interest is taxed by the state. The outcome depends on the investor's income tax bracket.

We discussed in Chapter One some of the factors that influence the yields of securities in general. Now let's look at some of the factors that, at any one time, could influence the yields on bills specifically. T-Bills tend to offer the lowest yields compared to the other money market securities. This is because bills are the most secure and the most liquid. The difference in yield between any two securities is commonly referred to as their "spread." Over a period of time, investors will notice that this spread between bills and other securities fluctuates. There are times when the spread between bills and, say, Euro CDs is very narrow compared to its normal relationship. For example, let's say that the normal relationship in yields between a bill and a Euro CD for any maturity is .75 percent. In other words, if bills are yielding 8 percent, Euro CDs should be yielding 8.75 percent. Now let's say that this spread narrows to .25 percent. So, bills are yielding 8 percent and Euro CDs are yielding 8.25 percent. In this case, bills are considered "cheap" relative to Euro CDs. This is because investors can purchase the safer and more liquid bill for almost the same yield as a Euro CD. On the other hand, there are times when this spread widens, causing bills to look expensive to investors. Investors then have more of an incentive to purchase Euro CDs because of their relatively higher yield.

What causes this spread to fluctuate? A very simplified explanation is the supply of and the demand for bills vis-a-vis other securities. Let's look at the supply side of the equation first. As we know, the Treasury issues new three- and six-month bills every week, and one-year bills every month. The amounts of these new issues are usually fairly stable and predictable. There are times, however, when the Treasury may issue much more or less than is normal.

Depending on the overall demand for bills, this could influence the overall price of these new issues. For example, the issuance of a new bill in an amount considered significantly less than normal would tend to put an upward pressure on its price.

Now let's look at the demand side of the equation. Bills are considered by investors to be a "safe haven." Investors tend to take refuge in bills in troubled times (e.g., a recession), troubled financial markets (e.g., after a stock market crash), troubled political times, or times of concern over the creditworthiness of privately owned institutions. In periods of trouble, investors want their money in securities with the characteristics of bills: short in maturity, secure, and liquid. They are more willing to forgo a higher return for the safety offered by bills. Therefore, during tough times the demand for bills is highest, driving up their price and thus driving down their yield.

Of course, during more stable periods investors become less concerned with safety and tend to invest in riskier securities that offer a higher return. This tends to reduce the demand for bills, the safest security, driving their price downward and their yield upward. At the same time, demand for riskier securities increases because they offer higher yields. This increase in demand tends to drive their prices upward and their yields downward. The net effect is a narrowing of the spread between bills and the other securities.

At times, it may be difficult to find, or expensive to buy, outstanding bills due to a lack of supply in the market. This lack of supply is a result of the fact that most investors purchase bills when they are first issued and hold on to them until maturity. Once again, smaller supply tends to put upward pressure on price. This is especially true after a bill's maturity is reduced to under sixty days. Not only is there a lack of supply of under sixty-day bills available in the market, but the demand for such short maturities is typically high among the investment community at any one time. This is because there is a considerably high percentage of investors who are either restricted to invest, or prefer to invest, in very short maturing securities.

There are two large investors of bills, who at any one time can put a large amount of upward or downward pressure on the price of any one particular bill, several bills, or the entire bill market. The direction of the pressure will be a function of whether these investors are buying or selling bills. The amount of pressure placed on the bills will be a function of how many bills are bought or sold.

The first investor of consequence is the Federal Reserve. To alter the supply of funds in the banking system, and thus interest rates, the Fed may buy or sell large quantities of a specific bill or bills. This is one of the tools used by the Fed to conduct monetary policy. Obviously, the Federal Reserve buying or selling large amounts of bills has an immediate impact on the supply of bills. If, for example, the Fed is buying bills, the supply available to investors is reduced, placing upward pressure on bill prices, forcing yields lower. Furthermore, seeing the Fed buying bills may induce other investors into the marketplace to buy bills, further driving up their price. Investors not only witness the supply of bills reduced, but may view this action as an indication of Fed policy. Believing that the Fed wants rates lower, some investors may expect yields on bills to fall in the near future and will therefore buy bills today before their yields fall.

Primary dealers in U.S. Government securities are required to transact with the Fed when called upon. The Fed will often call upon the dealers to buy or sell bills with them. When the Fed buys bills, for example, it must simultaneously pay for them. These funds used to pay for the bills are deposited at banks, thus injecting money into the banking system. This added supply of funds into the banking system tends to reduce interest rates. Conversely, the selling of bills by the Fed has the opposite effect on the supply of funds in the banking system. In this instance, the Fed will receive funds for their sale of bills. These funds must leave the banking system to pay the Fed. Thus, the reduced supply of funds in the banking system will tend to put upward pressure on interest rates.

The second large investor that can alter the price of bills is any one of the large investors in the following group: foreign central banks, municipalities, dealers, banks, money funds, corporations, and insurance companies. There are entities in this group that have the ability to buy and sell such large quantities, that their transactions significantly affect the supply of bills and therefore the market price. These investors transact bills for their portfolio and/or for speculation.

Specific events also can affect the demand for bills. An example of such an event is a tax payment date. Individuals must pay their federal and state taxes by April 15 of each year and companies must pay their taxes by the fifteenth day of certain months each quarter. Knowing that they will have to pay the government on a specific date, companies and individuals may take this amount, if available, and invest it in a bill maturing just before the tax payment date. Thus, they earn interest on this money in a secure investment until they must relinquish all or part of the funds to the government. This increases the demand for bills maturing immediately before a tax payment date and therefore puts upward pressure on their prices.

All of the above factors, separately or in conjunction with one another, can affect the price of a bill, along with the factors discussed in Chapter One which affect the prices of securities in general.

Now we have decided to purchase a bill. The next step is to call up a financial institution for a price quote. The investor should give the following information: the face amount of the transaction, the maturity date of the bill desired, and whether the transaction is a purchase or a sale. The request should go something like this, "I wish to purchase a $10,000 T-Bill maturing June 7, 1990." Another common way of requesting a price quote is, "Where would you offer $10,000 of the June 7, 1990 bills?" The salesperson at the institution then states the discount rate at which they are willing to sell the bills. The salesperson should say something like this, "We will sell you $10,000 T-Bills maturing June 7, 1990 at 7.57 percent." If the investor approves of the price, both parties agree to a settlement date and the transaction occurs. And finally, both parties will agree on how the transfer of ownership and funds will transpire.

Before or after the transaction is complete, the investor may request from the institution additional information about the investment. The investor may want to know the cost of the transaction, the amount of interest that will be earned if the bills are held to maturity, and the bills' yield to maturity. Let's go through an example to show how these are calculated.

Now let us assume that an investor wishes to purchase a $10,000 bill maturing in ninety days at a discount rate of 7.75 percent. The formula most often used to determine a bill's cost is:

Formula

$$\text{Discount Amount} = \frac{(\text{Face Value} \times \text{Discount Rate})}{360} \times \text{Number of days to maturity}$$

$$\text{Cost of Bill} = \text{Face Value} - \text{Discount Amount}$$

Example

$$\text{Discount Amount} = \frac{(\$10,000 \times 7.75\%)}{360} \times 90$$

$$\text{Discount Amount} = \frac{(\$775)}{360} \times 90$$

$$\text{Discount Amount} = \$193.75$$

$$\text{Cost} = \$10,000 - \$193.75$$

$$\text{Cost} = \$9,806.25$$

Formula to Determine Interest Earned at Maturity

$$\text{Interest Earned} = \text{Discount Amount}$$

Example

INTEREST EARNED = $193.75, or the difference between what the investor pays for the bill, $9,806.25, and what the investor receives at maturity, $10,000.

Assuming the investor is in the 25 percent federal income tax bracket (remember, bills are state-tax-free, so we do not have to account for state tax), how much will actually be kept after taxes?

To determine after-tax income, subtract the amount of tax on the earnings from the total interest earned.

Formula

$$\text{AFTER-TAX EARNINGS} = \text{Total Interest Earned} - (\text{Total Interest Earned} \times \text{Tax Rate})$$

Example

$$\text{AFTER-TAX EARNINGS} = \$193.75 - (\$193.75 \times 25\%)$$

$$\text{After-Tax Earnings} = \$193.75 - \$48.44$$

$$\text{After-Tax Earnings} = \$145.31$$

Formula to Determine Yield to Maturity

$$\text{YIELD TO MATURITY} = \frac{(\text{Face Amount} - \text{Discount Cost})}{\text{Discount Cost}} \times \frac{365}{\text{Days to Maturity}}$$

Example

$$\text{Yield to Maturity} = \frac{(\$10,000 - \$9,806.25)}{\$9,806.25} \times \frac{365}{90}$$

$$\text{Yield to Maturity} = \frac{(\$193.75)}{\$9,806.25} \times \frac{365}{90}$$

$$\text{Yield to Maturity} = .0197578 \times \frac{365}{90}$$

$$\text{Yield to Maturity} = .0801288 = 8.01\%$$

This formula is accurate in most instances for bills, but there are several circumstances when the above formula changes slightly. An investor who wants an exact yield to maturity for any security should use a yield table or bond calculator.

The yield used in the above example is referred to as a bond equivalent yield. As you can see, this formula assumes that a year contains 365 days. This yield is useful when comparing yields on other securities that are based on a 365-day year, such as yields on discount notes and other types of bonds. The yields on many other securities assume that a year contains 360 days (referred to as a CD or money market equivalent yield). Therefore, to accurately compare the yield on a bill to that of a security whose yield assumes a 360 day year, we must convert a bill's yield to a 360-day basis. Use the following formula to convert:

Formula to Convert a Bond Equivalent Yield to a CD Equivalent Yield

$$\text{CD EQUIVALENT YIELD} = \text{Bond Equivalent Yield} \times \frac{360}{365}$$

Using the above example:

$$\text{CD Equivalent Yield} = 8.01\% \times \frac{360}{365}$$

$$\text{CD Equivalent Yield} = .0790027 = 7.90\%$$

Let's say the investor decides to sell this $10,000 bill forty-five days before maturity. The investor receives a 7.25 percent bid price from the financial institution, which he accepts. How much money is received from the proceeds of the sale? How much was earned from the investment?

We can use the first formula to determine the discount amount. In the second formula, which determines the cost of a bill, we can substitute "cost" for "proceeds received from the sale."

Formula

$$\text{Discount Amount} = \frac{(\text{Face Value} \times \text{Discount Rate})}{360} \times \text{Number of days to maturity}$$

$$\text{Proceeds from Sale} = \text{Face Value} - \text{Discount Amount}$$

Example

$$\text{Discount Amount} = \frac{(\$10{,}000 \times 7.25\%)}{360} \times 45$$

$$\text{Discount Amount} = \frac{(725)}{360} \times 45$$

$$\text{Discount Amount} = \$90.63$$

$$\text{Proceeds from Sale} = \$10{,}000 - \$90.63$$

$$\text{Proceeds from Sale} = \$9{,}909.37$$

To determine how much money was earned from the sale, subtract the cost of the original purchase from the proceeds of the sale.

Formula

$$\text{Amount Earned from the Sale} = \text{Proceeds of Sale} - \text{Cost of Purchase}$$

Example

$$\text{Amount Earned} = \$9{,}909.37 - \$9{,}806.25$$

$$\text{Amount Earned} = \$103.12$$

The reader should realize that two factors went into producing $103.12 in earnings. The first factor is that the investor held the bill for forty-five days, thus earning interest for the period. In addition, the bill appreciated in price during the forty-five days held, from the original purchase discount of 7.75 percent to the selling discount of 7.25 percent.

OK, now it is your turn. Given the following information, determine the bill's cost, interest earned at maturity, interest earned after taxes, bond equivalent yield, and CD equivalent yield.

An investor wants to purchase a $25,000 bill that matures in 180 days at a discount of 8 percent. Assume that the investor is in the 28 percent federal tax bracket. The answers, along with explanations, are in Appendix A at the end of the book.

COST

INTEREST EARNED AT MATURITY

BOND EQUIVALENT YIELD

CD EQUIVALENT YIELD

The investor decides to sell the $25,000 bill with 135 days left to maturity. The selling rate received from the financial institution is 7.72 percent. What are the proceeds and earnings from the sale?

Chapter 2

PROCEEDS

EARNINGS

Chapter Three

UNITED STATES GOVERNMENT AGENCY DISCOUNT NOTES

United States government agency discount notes are typically referred to in the marketplace simply as "discount notes" or "agencies." Sometimes investors will hear these securities called "discos." Discount notes are the short-term obligations of federally sponsored agencies that supply credit to specific sectors of the economy. The discount notes discussed in this chapter will be those of the Federal Farm Credit Bank (FFCB), Federal Home Loan Bank (FHLB), Federal National Mortgage Corporation (FNMA), and Federal Home Loan Mortgage Corporation (FHLMC). The primary function of the FHLB, FNMA, and FHLMC is to provide funds for mortgages. The primary function of the FFCB is to provide funds for farmers. One way these agencies acquire funds to lend to these sectors is issuing discount notes to the public.

Discount notes are among the most popular money market securities purchased by investors today. The features which make them attractive to investors are a relatively high degree of safety (low default risk), a relatively high degree of liquidity, favorable tax features (in some cases), low minimum denominations, and higher yields than T-Bills across the maturity spectrum.

Discount notes are purchased on a discount basis. Once again, the investor pays less than the stated face value of the security at the time of purchase and receives the face value at maturity. This can be helpful to the investor who may not have the full face value to invest at the time of purchase. Another attractive feature of discount notes is that they are transacted in book-entry form. As has been stated, this frees the investor from safekeeping a negotiable certificate. It also enables the investor to wire the discount notes to his chosen record-keeping institution, while actually doing the transacting with any firm.

Both discount notes and T-Bills have these features, but there are differences between the two. The major difference is that T-Bills are guaranteed by the U.S. government and thus are considered the safest instrument available. Discount notes are guaranteed by the issuing agency and thus are tied to the creditworthiness of their respective agency. However, because these agencies are sponsored by the federal government, they are considered a moral obligation of the federal government. The marketplace perceives that should any of the agencies incur financial difficulties, the federal government would step in to help, thereby avoiding default. In the history of these agencies there has never been a default. The general opinion in the marketplace is that U.S. government agency discount notes are among the safest securities available. But, because they are not full faith and credit obligations of the U.S. government, some investors shy away from these issues. As a result, discount notes are offered at higher yields than T-Bills. This goes back to what we learned in Chapter One: investors must be compensated for the perception of higher risk. Many investors find these higher yields sufficient incentive to forgo a stated government guarantee. As with everything else, the investor determines how important a stated federal government guarantee is and if the higher yield is adequate compensation for the higher risk.

Discount notes are among the most liquid securities available. A large and organized secondary market exists in these securities, providing investors with the ability to convert their investment into cash easily. Discount notes, however, are not considered as liquid an investment as T-Bills, mainly because there are more T-Bills than discount notes outstanding. In 1989, the U.S. Treasury issued more than twice as many short-term securities as FHLB, FNMA, FHLMC, and FFCB combined. In 1989, the U.S. Treasury auctioned approximately $1 trillion in T-Bills. The combined total amount of discount notes issued by the four agencies in 1989 was under $500 billion.[1] Another reason why T-Bills are more liquid is that there are more investors of T-Bills than discount notes, so the secondary market for discount notes has less depth than that for bills. The investor should realize that liquidity is relative: investors will always be able to cash in their agencies before maturity, should the need arise. However, because discount notes are considered less liquid than bills, discount note yields are higher than T-Bill yields.

Some general features of a discount note are the same for each type of agency security discussed in this chapter. For example, all discount notes mature in one year or less. All discount notes are first issued by their respective agency and sold through a specific group of authorized dealers. Investors can purchase newly issued agencies either directly through these dealers or through another financial institution, which purchases the securities from an authorized dealer. All "discos" are purchased on a discount basis and issued in book entry form.

There are differences among each of the agency discount notes. For example, there are differences in minimum denomination, maturity range, taxation, guarantees, and perceived creditworthiness. Let us look at each type of agency discount note in detail.

Federal Farm Credit Bank discount notes are issued by a private, cooperatively owned, government-chartered system of banks and associations. This agency provides mortgage loans, short- and intermediate-term credit, and related services to farmers, ranchers, and other related businesses. FFCB discount notes (known in the market as "Farm Credits") are backed by all of the Farm Credit Banks in the U.S. No liability is assumed by the U.S. government. The market assumes a moral obligation on the part of the federal government to back FFCB discount notes should a problem arise.

---

1 Information provided by the U.S. Treasury and the four agencies.

Federal Home Loan Bank discount notes (known in the market as "Home Loans") are issued by the Federal Home Loan Bank System. This system was set up as a central reserve system for the savings and loan, or thrift, industry. Its goal is to ensure the availability of funds to the public for home financing. FHLB's primary source of funds is the issuance of bonds and discount notes. FHLB discount notes are guaranteed by the combined assets of the twelve regional Federal Home Loan Banks. They are also indirectly backed by the assets of the FHLB's member thrift institutions. Similar to FFCB discount notes, the federal government assumes no liability for these securities. But, because they are a U.S. government agency issue, the market perceives that the government has a moral obligation to back FHLB discount notes. With many savings and loan associations, and the Federal Home Loan Bank System having serious financial difficulties of late, the federal government's moral obligation is being tested. Congress has passed legislation authorizing the issuance of new government-backed securities and increases in the amount of regular government securities, the proceeds of which are funneled to the ailing entities. Although there have been many changes enacted of late in regards to the savings and loan industry, the characteristics of, and the way FHLB Discount Notes are handled, has remained the same.

Federal National Mortgage Association discount notes are issued by the Federal National Mortgage Association (FNMA or "Fannie Mae"). Fannie Mae is a government-sponsored agency set up to provide liquidity to the home mortgage market. It issues securities and uses the funds to purchase FHA-insured, VA-guaranteed, and conventional mortgages from mortgage lenders. With the proceeds received from the sale of mortgages to FNMA, the lenders originate new home mortgages. Fannie Mae also purchases mortgages and resells them in the form of guaranteed securities. FNMA discount notes are not direct obligations of the federal government, but rather are unsecured general obligations of Fannie Mae.

Federal Home Loan Mortgage Corporation discount notes are issued by the Federal Home Loan Mortgage Corporation (FHLMC or "Freddie Mac"). Like Fannie Mae, Freddie Mac was set up to improve the liquidity of home mortgages. Freddie Mac purchases FHA/VA and conventional mortgage loans from mortgage lenders for resale in the form of guaranteed securities. Upon selling their loans to FHLMC, the lending institutions can originate new mortgages. One way Freddie Mac funds its operation is through the issuance of discount notes, which are unsecured general obligations of FHLMC and not direct obligations of the federal government. There is virtually no difference between the functions performed by FNMA and FHLMC. In practice, Fannie Mae holds a larger portion of its purchased mortgages in its own portfolio than does Freddie Mac.

Agency discount notes are offered to the public in various minimum denominations. Farm Credit discount notes are issued with a minimum face value of $5,000; over $5,000, investors may purchase them in increments of $5,000. In other words, they may be purchased in amounts of $10,000, $15,000, $20,000, and so forth. Home Loan discount notes are issued in minimum denominations of $100,000; over this minimum, they may be purchased in increments of $5,000. Fannie Mae discount notes are issued in minimum denominations of $10,000 and additional increments of $5,000. Freddie Mac discount notes are issued in minimum denominations of $25,000 and additional increments of $1,000. Remember, for all these securities, the investor actually pays an amount less than the face value received at maturity.

Discount notes also come in various maturities. Farm Credit notes range in maturity from five days to one year. Fannie Mae and Home Loan discount notes range in maturity from thirty to 360 days. Freddie Mac discount notes mature on a variety of dates one year or less from issuance.

Only two of the four types of discount notes offer investors the same tax advantage as T Bills. The interest earned on FFCB and FHLB discount notes are taxed only by the federal government, as with bills. Interest earned on FNMA and FHLMC discount notes, however, is taxed by the federal, state, and local governments. This can be an important factor in choosing between the various agency notes.

Newly issued discount notes are brought to the marketplace in a very different way than are bills. Every day each agency will post offering rates on their discount notes for various maturities within one year. These offerings are considered primary or newly issued securities. Investors may obtain these from one of the dealers authorized to sell that agency's newly issued securities. If the institution that you are doing business with is not part of this selling group, it can purchase them for you at the agency's posted rate for that maturity.

Here is an example. Let's say that the FHLB is posting the following rates: 30-60 days at 7.75 percent, 60-90 days at 7.85 percent, 90-120 days at 7.80 percent, 120-180 days at 7.60 percent, and 180-360 days at 7.50 percent. The FHLB is willing to issue new discount notes to the public at these discount rates. So, for example, if an investor wishes to purchase a Home Loan maturing 92 days from today, the discount rate price of this newly issued security will be 7.80 percent. Once an agency has attracted the amount of funds needed for that day, they typically remove their rates from the market, accepting no more funds. When this occurs, investors say, "The Window is Closed."

Investors may also purchase discount notes in the secondary market through financial institutions. It is often difficult to find discount notes with a specific single maturity date in the secondary market. Hence, the investor may receive from his institution various quotes on discount notes maturing near the date(s) sought. The rate quoted by the institution is not determined by the specific agency but by the marketplace and the selling institution. An example of a price quote on a discount note is, "A $50,000 FFCB discount note maturing June 11,1990 at a discount rate of 7.95 percent."

Whether buying or selling, the investor has to tell the salesperson at his financial institution which agency's discount note is to be transacted, the face amount of the security, and the maturity date (or preferred maturity date). At this time, the investor learns from the salesperson either the discount rate at which the institution is willing to buy or sell the notes or the discount rate that the agency is quoting "at the window." If this price is acceptable to the investor, the transaction is completed. Settlement for newly issued discount notes typically occurs the same day (cash settlement). Settlement for previously issued notes occurs on the date agreed upon by the buyer and the seller, typically the next business day (regular settlement).

United States Government Agency Discount Notes

Certainly the factors influencing the prices of all securities affect discount notes, as do the supply and demand factors discussed in Chapter One. And, some of the factors that determine the price of bills (discussed in Chapter Two) also can come into play with discount notes. For example, a factor such as the proximity of a note's maturity date to a tax payment can be most important in determining price. Because the moral backing of the federal government is associated with discount notes, many investors purchase them during periods when safety is a major concern. Obviously, more investors purchasing discount notes tends to drive up their price. But, there are two factors unique to discount notes that have a direct effect on their pricing. The rates on new issues are determined by each agency daily, and the securities are guaranteed by a federal agency with the moral backing of the federal government.

As described above, every day each agency will post a series of rates for various maturities through one year. These rates represent at what rate the agency is willing to borrow funds. Part of what determines the rate offered by each agency is, of course, the general trend in interest rates. However, the factors which determine the exact rates offered are unique to each agency. For example, one very important factor is the amount of funds the agency needs for operations on that day. If the agency needs a significantly higher amount of funds on any day, it might post a higher level of rates in the hope of attracting more investors. Similarly, if the need is not great the agency might offer a lower, less attractive rate. Of course, once the funding needs for the day are satisfied the agency can remove its rates from the marketplace.

The agency may need to attract investor funds over a specific time horizon. Yes, the agency wants to attract "X" amount of funds today. But it may need more funds for thirty days than for ninety days. The agency may need more funds for a certain time period to meet an anticipated financial need during that time period. Or, the agency may adjust its offer based on expected interest rate movements. For example, if the agency feels that rates will be rising soon they may be more inclined to try to attract longer-term funds to minimize borrowing costs. So, their longer maturity rates today may be relatively high in order to attract investors. In this case the agency feels that whatever rate it will pay investors today will be cheap compared to the higher rates that may be needed to attract funds tomorrow. The reverse is true if the agency expects rates to go down: the agency will post higher short-term rates. This way, when these investments come due, they can issue more discount notes at lower rates and thus a lower cost to the agency.

Earlier in this chapter, we discussed how the market perception of the safety and liquidity of discount notes influences the price of agencies vis-a-vis bills. We stated that because discount notes are considered slightly less safe and liquid than bills, they offer higher yields than bills. But they generally yield less than the other money market securities because they are backed by a government agency, are considered to have the moral backing of the federal government, and have a large secondary market. In later chapters we will learn that many of the other securities either do not have as large secondary market or do not have the implicit backing of the federal government. Thus, investors need to be compensated by receiving a higher yield, if they are to buy the other securities.

Investors will find that throughout history, the yield differential between discount notes and other securities has fluctuated. One factor that has greatly influenced this spread over the past few years has been the financial status of the various agencies. None of these agencies has ever defaulted on its debt securities nor are any defaults expected in the future. During the 1980s, there was a significant amount of bad press in regard to the financial condition of the agencies mentioned in this chapter. Any bad financial news about a debt-issuing entity tends to dissuade investors from buying their securities. As we already have learned, when the demand for a security goes down, its yield must go up to attract investors. And there have been times when bad financial results made yields on an agency's discount notes move higher. Furthermore, when an entity goes through periods of hard financial times, it usually needs more funds to help with the problems. This increased demand for funds exacerbates the upward pressure on the issuer's rates.

Having decided to purchase an agency discount note, the investor must call a financial institution to obtain a rate quote. The investor tells the salesperson the specific date of maturity sought or a range of dates that is acceptable for maturity. So let's say the

United States Government Agency Discount Notes

investor wants to purchase a Fannie Mae discount note. The request to the salesperson should go something like this, "I wish to purchase a $25,000 Fannie Mae discount note maturing September 29, 1990." The salesperson then states the discount price at which the institution is willing to sell the note. This is either a price quote on an outstanding note or the rate at which the agency is willing to issue a new note ("at the window"). The salesperson says something like, "We will sell you $25,000 FNMA discount notes maturing on September 29, 1990 at 8.25 percent." If the investor approves of this rate and the proposed settlement date, the transaction occurs. Both parties will then agree where the notes are to be held for safekeeping and how funds will be transferred for payment.

Now let's use this example to determine the cost of the transaction, the amount of interest earned if held to maturity, and the yield to maturity. Let's assume that September 29, the maturity date, is 270 days from the date of purchase. The formulas used to determine these figures for discount notes are identical to those used for T-Bills so let's go through this example as a way of practicing what we already know.

The formula used to determine the cost of a discount note is:

Formula

$$\text{Discount Amount} = \frac{(\text{Face Value} \times \text{Discount Rate})}{360} \times \text{Number of days to maturity}$$

$$\text{Cost of Discount Note} = \text{Face Value} - \text{Discount Amount}$$

Example

$$\text{Discount Amount} = \frac{(\$25,000 \times 8.25\%)}{360} \times 270$$

$$\text{Discount Amount} = \frac{(\$2,062.50)}{360} \times 270$$

$$\text{Discount Amount} = \$1{,}546.88$$

$$\text{Cost} = \$25{,}000 - \$1{,}546.88$$

$$\text{Cost} = \$23{,}453.12$$

Formula to Determine Interest Earned if Held to Maturity

$$\text{INTEREST EARNED} = \text{Discount Amount}$$

Example

Interest Earned = $1,546.88, or the difference between what the investor pays for the FNMA discount note, $23,453.12, and what the investor receives at maturity, $25,000.

Now let's take taxes into account. Remember, the income earned on FNMA discount notes is taxed by both the federal and state governments (for the sake of this example we will ignore local taxes). Assume that the investor is in the 20 percent federal and 10 percent state income tax brackets. So, how much will the investor earn after taxes? Remember, to determine after-tax income, subtract the amount of tax on earnings from the total interest earned.

Formula

$$\text{After-Tax Earnings} = \text{Total Interest Earned} - \left(\text{Total Interest Earned} \times \text{Tax Rate}\right)$$

Example

$$\text{After-Tax Earnings} = \$1{,}546.88 - (\$1{,}546.88 \times 20\%) - (\$1{,}546.88 \times 10\%)$$

United States Government Agency Discount Notes

After-Tax Earnings = $1,546.88 − $309.38 − $154.69

After-Tax Earnings = $1,082.81

Formula to Determine Yield to Maturity

$$\text{Yield to Maturity} = \frac{(\text{Face Amount} - \text{Discount Cost})}{\text{Discount Cost}} \times \frac{365}{\text{days to maturity}}$$

Example

$$\text{Yield to Maturity} = \frac{(\$25{,}000 - \$23{,}453.12)}{\$23{,}453.12} \times \frac{365}{270}$$

$$\text{Yield to Maturity} = \frac{(\$1{,}546.88)}{\$23{,}453.12} \times \frac{365}{270}$$

$$\text{Yield to Maturity} = .0659562 \times \frac{365}{270}$$

$$\text{Yield to Maturity} = .089163 = 8.92 \text{ percent}$$

Remember that this formula is accurate in most instances for discount notes; there are various circumstances in which it changes slightly. An investor who needs the exact yield to maturity for all cases should use a yield table or bond calculator.

As you will recall, the above yield is referred to as a bond equivalent yield. The investor can use this yield to accurately compare this discount note to other discount notes or to T-Bills. Now let's say we want to compare this yield to a security whose yield is computed as a money market (or CD) yield. To do this for the discount note, we use the exact same formula as that used for a T-Bill. Let's use the example we have been using to practice.

Formula to Convert a Bond Equivalent Yield into a CD Equivalent Yield

$$\frac{\text{CD Equivalent Yield}}{} = \text{Bond Equivalent Yield} \times \frac{360}{365}$$

Example

$$\text{CD Equivalent Yield} = 8.92\% \times \frac{360}{365}$$

$$\text{CD Equivalent Yield} = .087978 = 8.80 \text{ percent}$$

Now let's say the investor decides to sell this $25,000 FNMA discount note ninety days from maturity. The investor receives a 7.75 percent bid price from the financial institution and accepts it. How much money will the investor receive from the sale? How much money was earned from the sale? We will use the same method that we used for T-Bills.

Formula

$$\text{Discount Amount} = \frac{(\text{Face Amount} \times \text{Discount Rate})}{360} \times \text{Number of Days to maturity}$$

Proceeds From the Sale = Face Amount − Discount Amount

Example

$$\text{Discount Amount} = \frac{(\$25{,}000 \times 7.75\%)}{360} \times 90$$

$$\text{Discount Amount} = \frac{(\$1{,}937.50)}{360} \times 90$$

Discount Amount = $484.38

United States Government Agency Discount Notes

$$\text{Proceeds From Sale} = \$25{,}000 - \$484.38$$

$$\text{Proceeds From Sale} = \$24{,}515.62$$

Once again, to determine how much money was earned from this investment use the following formula:

Formula

$$\text{Amount Earned From the Investment} = \text{Proceeds of Sale} - \text{Cost of Purchase}$$

Example

$$\text{Amount Earned From the Investment} = \$24{,}515.62 - \$23{,}453.12$$

$$\text{Amount Earned From the Investment} = \$1{,}062.50$$

OK, now you take over. Using the following example, determine the discount note's cost, interest earned if the security is held to maturity, interest earned after taxes, bond equivalent yield and CD equivalent yield.

An investor wants to purchase a $75,000 FHLMC discount note maturing in sixty-three days at a discount rate of 7.87 percent. Assume that the investor is in the 25 percent federal and 12 percent state income tax brackets. The answers are in Appendix A.

COST

INTEREST EARNED AT MATURITY

BOND EQUIVALENT YIELD

United States Government Agency Discount Notes 57

CD EQUIVALENT YIELD

The investor decides to sell the discount note with thirty-two days left to maturity. The selling price received from the financial institution is 7.61 percent. How much is received from the sale? What are the earnings from this investment?

PROCEEDS

EARNINGS

Chapter Four

TIME DEPOSITS OF FINANCIAL INSTITUTIONS

Time deposits of financial institutions originate when investors lend money to financial institutions. An understanding exists between the investor and the institution that after an agreed upon period of time, the institution will return to the investor the "deposited" principal along with earned interest. For financial institutions, these instruments are among the most important sources of funding for operations. There are several types of time deposits available today. This chapter will deal with the most popular ones: negotiable certificates of deposit, negotiable Eurodollar certificates of deposit, and Eurodollar time deposits.

Probably the time deposit that is most familiar to investors is the certificate of deposit, or CD. When most people think of CDs, they think of going to their local bank and depositing a specific amount of money for a stated period of time and rate of return. This type of CD is referred to as a non-negotiable CD. Non-negotiable CDs, however, are not a major source of funds for banks. They are typically small in size, offer no secondary market, and may be subject to various rules and restrictions (depending on the institution). In addition to non-negotiable CDs, institutions may issue another type of time deposit, which is typically larger in size, known as a negotiable CD. The negotiable CD is a major source of funding for financial institutions and will be discussed in this chapter.

Negotiable CDs, are an obligation of a bank or other financial institutions. The bank promises to repay principal plus interest on funds left on deposit at the institution for a specific period of time. When a CD is newly issued it is referred to as a primary CD. Beyond the guarantee of the issuing bank, the Federal Deposit Insurance Corporation, a government entity, insures CDs issued by their member institutions (mainly banks). The Savings Association Insurance Fund (SAIF) provides comparable insurance on CDs issued by its members (mainly savings and loan associations).

As the name suggests, negotiable CDs are issued in a bearer negotiable certificate form. As you know, the certificates contain the terms of the deposit but do not contain the investor's name so they can be converted easily to cash. To minimize risk of theft or fraud, investors need to have a financial institution safekeep these negotiable certificates.

Many investors allow the financial institution issuing the CD to safekeep the certificates. However, many other investors, especially those large in size, have another institution safekeep the CDs. To facilitate this, large CDs are issued in New York. This has proven to be convenient because often times investors and issuers of CDs are in different cities. Many large buyers of CDs (and other products) have a financial institution in New York to act as safekeeping agent. Then, when a CD is purchased the investor may request to have the certificates delivered from the issuer in New York to their safekeeping agent, also in New York.

Although most are issued in bearer form, CDs may also be issued in registered form. In fact, all CDs that mature in over eighteen months must be registered in the owner's name. A purchaser of CDs maturing in less than eighteen months may request to have the certificates registered. However, should the investor try to liquidate the CD before maturity, registered CDs must be de-registered (thereby becoming negotiable) before they can be sold in the marketplace. Depending on the institution and the circumstances, some institutions may allow early redemption of the CD, in the event of the need for liquidation.

Another popular type of CD is the negotiable Eurodollar certificate of deposit, or Euro CD for short. Euro CDs are a negotiable, bearer, U.S. dollar-denominated certificate of deposit that are issued outside the U.S. They are issued either by a foreign branch of a U.S. bank or by a foreign bank. U.S. investors refer to Euro CDs issued by branches of U.S. banks as domestic Euro CDs, and Euro CDs issued by non-U.S. banks as foreign Euro CDs. Two examples of Euro CD issuers are a Citibank branch in London (domestic Euro CD) and a Fuji Bank branch in London (foreign Euro CD).

Both types of Euro CDs are backed by the parent bank of the issuing branch or bank. Euro CDs are not insured by any insurance agency, so the issuer is the sole guarantor of a Euro CD. As you will find out later in this chapter, Euro CDs offer a higher yield than standard CDs issued by U.S.-based institutions (sometimes called domestic CDs). The lack of insurance is just one factor that influences the yield differential.

Theoretically, Euro CDs can be issued anywhere outside the U.S., but most are issued in London. Because Euro CDs are issued in a negotiable, bearer form, London serves as the central place of issuance and delivery, just as New York serves the domestic CD market. Although Euro CDs are issued outside the U.S., the investor's money never actually leaves the U.S. Even so, the investor should consider the political risk of the country in which the certificate is issued, typically the United Kingdom. Of course with the U.K.'s long history of political and social stability, the investor really need not worry. In fact, Euro CDs are considered safe investments by most investors.

Eurodollar time deposits (Euro time deposits, or Euro TDs for short) are U.S. dollars deposited for a stated maturity and rate of return. The deposit is placed outside the U.S., either in a foreign bank or in a foreign branch of a U.S. bank. Most U.S. banks issue their Euro TDs out of their Nassau or Cayman Island branches. When an investor purchases a Euro TD, the invested funds never actually leave the country. The security is issued by the bank as a book-entry deposit and posted on the books of their "off-shore" branch. These deposits are backed by the issuing branch's parent bank. There is no FDIC insurance on Euro TDs.

The vast majority of time deposits are issued on an interest bearing basis as opposed to a discount basis. In this case, investors purchase the security at its face value and receive a stated rate of interest on the security's face value. For example, let's say an investor purchases a $500,000 CD from a U.S. bank to mature in thirty days at an interest rate of 8 percent. The investor deposits (purchases the security for) $500,000, and thirty days later receives $500,000 plus thirty days of 8 percent annual interest on $500,000. If a CD matures in one year or more, interest is typically paid to the investor semiannually. CDs can also be purchased on a discount basis similar to bills and discount notes. These CDs are referred to as zero coupon CDs.

The vast majority of time deposits are issued with a fixed rate of interest. A fixed-rated security earns the same interest rate over the life of the instrument. There are time deposits available that offer a floating rate of interest, or variable-rate CDs. With variable-rate CDs, the issuer and depositor agree at the time of purchase that after a certain period of time during the life of the security, the rate of interest will be adjusted. The two parties also must agree how the new rate will be determined. Typically, this rate is adjusted off of an agreed to index rate. Some examples of indices used to determine adjustable rates are the Federal Reserve composite CD rate, the prime rate, LIBOR (London Interbank Offering Rate), a commercial paper index, a T-Bill auction rate, and a stock market index. Here is an example of how the adjustment works. Let's say an investor purchases for $1,000,000 a six-month variable-rate CD. Both the issuer and investor have agreed that every thirty days the rate which the investor earns will adjust to five basis points above the thirty-day LIBOR rate. Thirty days from now, at the time to readjust the investor's rate, the thirty day LIBOR rate is at 8.50 percent. So, for the next thirty days, the investor will receive an 8.55 percent return on his investment of $1,000,000.

There are no legal minimum denominations for any of the time deposits discussed here. Each institution can declare its own minimum denomination, but most institutions establish similar policies. Typically, the smallest minimum denomination available on a negotiable CD is $100,000. Many issuers find it more cost-effective to issue certificates in amounts greater than $100,000. Usually any incremental amount over the minimum denomination is acceptable. The investor needs to consult the issuer to determine its rules for minimum denominations and additional increments.

Investors will find that to obtain a Euro CD or domestic CD in the secondary market, they must purchase a minimum of $1,000,000. In fact, $5,000,000 is more commonplace. The reason for this is quite simple. Most small investors of CDs will purchase newly issued CDs and hold them to maturity, so there are not many negotiable CDs under $1,000,000 in the secondary market. Similarly, there are not many investors seeking small amounts of time deposits in the secondary market. There are many large investors (pension managers, municipalities, corporations), however, who are willing buyers of secondary CDs (if the price is right). These investors also are more apt to liquidate time deposits that they have purchased in order to meet cash flow needs. These investors tend to deal in amounts of $1,000,000, $5,000,000, and up, so there is a large secondary market for these larger time deposits.

Investors will also find that the typical minimum denomination in the marketplace for primary or secondary Euro CDs is $5,000,000. Issuers have found it more practical to issue their Euro CDs in minimum amounts of this size, with increments of $5,000,000 because most of the investors in this instrument are very large. However, investors will find that there are times when an institution will "break up" an outstanding Euro CD of $5,000,000 and sell it in smaller amounts. Typically, these smaller amounts are in increments of $1,000,000.

Investors will find that most institutions offer Euro time deposits for a minimum of $100,000 and any incremental amount over the minimum. But once again, investors should consult with the issuing institution to ascertain the policy regarding the minimum and increments.

Newly issued domestic CDs can be issued with maturities of seven days to five years. Theoretically, CDs can mature in more than five years, but this is rare and is typically done through a private placement. The majority of CDs are issued to mature in thirty days to six months. There are very rarely any secondary CDs that mature in under thirty days: once a security has less than thirty days to mature, most investors will hold it to maturity. Hence the supply of these short-maturity instruments in the secondary market is small.

Euro CDs range in maturity from thirty days to five years. Like CDs, however, the majority of Euro CDs issued and traded have maturities of thirty to 180 days.

Euro TDs can be issued to mature as early as the next business day. In fact, many investors find Euro TDs to be a very attractive overnight investment compared with other securities with one-day terms. Euro TDs can also mature in several years, similar to the other time deposits. The most common Euro TDs mature between one day and six months.

Time deposits do not carry the same tax advantages as T-Bills or some discount notes. When an investor purchases a time deposit, earned interest income is subject to federal, state, and local taxes. These tax rates are determined by the investor's particular circumstances.

Newly issued time deposits come to the market in almost the same way as newly issued discount notes. Typically each day, financial institutions set interest rates at which they are willing to accept funds for specific time periods. Not every institution offers all the various types of time deposits or in every maturity. While discount notes are sold to the public through an authorized group of dealers, time deposits are typically sold directly by the issuing institution. Some institutions, however, do sell their time deposits through one or more dealers. Either way, the investor simply picks the maturity date and will receive as interest the rate posted for that maturity by that institution. Many investors find this feature very appealing. After all, being able to pick the specific date of maturity is advantageous in satisfying cash flow needs and/or interest rate movement expectations.

The rates received on these time deposits are affected by the factors influencing the rates on other debt securities, as described in Chapter One. The rates on time deposits at a particular moment are determined by the overall level of short term interest rates and by the market for the type of security being purchased. The strategy used by financial institutions to determine their rates on newly issued deposits resembles that used by agencies for their discount notes. As described in Chapter Three, a combination of the institution's need for funds and its expectations for the direction of interest rates directly influences the rates that it will quote. Another very important factor influencing the rates offered by a particular institution is the institution's perceived creditworthiness. The market's perception reflects not only default risk but also liquidity. Obviously, the less creditworthy an institution, the higher its overall rates must be in order to attract investors.

Financial institution deposits always offer higher yields than T-Bills or discount notes because investors perceive that the federal government and federal government agencies are safer than any financial institution. And, the secondary markets for time deposits are not considered as broad as those for T-Bills and discount notes. So once again, investors need to be compensated through a higher return for the perception of higher risk. But, to many investors obtaining the highest yield available, in and of itself, is very appealing.

Although they are considered a higher risk relative to T-Bills and discount notes, time deposits of major financial institutions are considered among the safest instruments available. They typically have short maturities and therefore are considered to be safe by the very nature of their short lives. Investors can research the institutions to determine which ones they feel comfortable investing in. Remember, rating agencies exist to provide their analysis on the financial condition of institutions, to help investors with this process. Every institution has its own financial record, business focus, and so on. Whether or not an individual invests in any particular institution depends on his level of comfort with this background information. In any case, the investor must consider the creditworthiness of the issuing institution because it is the ultimate guarantor of the investment.

The matter of time deposits having a smaller secondary market than bills and discount notes is also one of relativity. In fact, one of the major appeals of CDs and Euro CDs is their liquidity. These securities are issued in bearer, negotiable form, and a large and organized secondary market exists for both. Therefore, should the investor need to liquidate before maturity, he can easily do so. True, deposits are not considered to have as broad a secondary market as T-Bills or discount notes because of the smaller size of the issues outstanding and the smaller number of investors and market makers in these products. But, the investment community considers the secondary market to be large enough to make CDs and Euro CDs liquid. The investor should realize that typically the larger and more financially strong an institution is, the more liquid its debt securities. Obviously, there are more investors willing to buy securities from larger, more secure and well-known institutions. This directly influences a security's yield.

Euro CDs and Euro TDs typically offer investors higher yields than domestic CDs, and for many investors this makes them more appealing than domestic CDs. One reason for the higher yields is the perception that dollars deposited outside the U.S. are riskier than those deposited inside the U.S. This perception is partly due to the fact that Euro CD issuing banks are not as tightly regulated as U.S. banks. Furthermore, U.S. bank deposits are insured by the FDIC for up to $100,000 while Euros are not insured by the FDIC or any other agency. Also, because there are fewer outstanding issues and investors of Euro CDs relative to domestic CDs, a smaller secondary market exists. Euro TDs do not even have a secondary market. In fact, some institutions have penalties for the early liquidation of Euro TDs. Therefore, Euros are not considered as liquid as domestic CDs. So once again, investors must be enticed, through a higher return, to take on additional risk.

As has been stated, investors may purchase domestic CDs and Euro CDs in the secondary market. These purchases can be made through the investor's financial institution. The difficulty of obtaining a secondary CD or Euro CD with a specific maturity date, issued by a specific institution, is a function of the supply in the secondary market at that time. Because it is often difficult to meet such specific requirements, an investor who wants to purchase a secondary deposit should request a range of acceptable maturities and issuers.

After making the request, the investor receives from the dealer interest rate price quotes on one or several secondary deposits that match the parameters set. This secondary market quote is not determined by the issuing institution, but rather how other secondary deposits with that maturity and perceived issuer creditworthiness are being traded in the marketplace. This quote is further influenced by the dealer's own business needs. The price quoted by the institution's salesperson will sound something like, "We can offer you a $5,000,000 Bankers' Trust CD that matures on July 18, 1990, has an originally issued coupon rate of 7.90 percent, was originally issued on January 29, 1990 at a price of 7.50 percent."

Whether buying or selling a newly issued or secondary market time deposit, the investor should give the salesperson the same information. He should state the face amount, the name of issuer (or issuers acceptable, if purchasing), the maturity date (or acceptable range of maturity dates), the original coupon rate (if selling), the original date of issuance (if selling), and how funds and the certificates are to be exchanged. At this time, the investor will be told either the rate that institution is quoting for newly issued deposits or the price the institution is willing to buy or sell a specific secondary issue. If this price is acceptable to the investor, the transaction is completed. Settlement for the purchase and sale of CDs, and the purchase of Euro TDs, can usually take place the same or the next business day. Settlement for the purchase and sale of Euro CDs usually takes place two business days after the transaction because of the time difference between London and the U.S. Settlement may take place earlier if the certificates need not be delivered. On settlement day, funds and the ownership of the securities are transferred as agreed by the buyer and seller.

Let's now go through an example to determine the purchase cost, interest earned at maturity, and yield to maturity when an investor purchases a newly issued deposit. The method of determining these is identical for CDs, Euro CDs and Euro TDs. In this example, we will use a Euro Time Deposit. The investor wishes to purchase a $100,000 Euro TD to mature in thirty days. The salesperson states that the institution is offering 8 percent for a Euro TD maturing in thirty days. To determine the cost of this deposit use the following formula:

Formula for the Cost of an Interest Bearing Deposit

$$\text{Cost} = \text{Face Value}$$

Example

$$\text{Cost} = \$100{,}000$$

The cost of an interest bearing deposit is simply its face value. In this example, the face value, and cost, is $100,000.

Formula to Determine Interest Earned on an Interest-Bearing Deposit

$$\frac{\text{Interest}}{\text{Earned}} = \frac{(\text{Principal} \times \text{Rate})}{360} \times \frac{\text{Number of Days}}{\text{to maturity}}$$

* Please note that sometimes institutions will calculate interest based on a 365 day year. In those cases, substitute 365 for 360 in the above formula.

Example

$$\frac{\text{Interest}}{\text{Earned}} = \frac{(\$100{,}000 \times 8\%)}{360} \times 30$$

$$\frac{\text{Interest}}{\text{Earned}} = \frac{(\$8{,}000)}{360} \times 30$$

$$\text{Interest Earned} = \$666.67$$

Remember, the interest earned on Euro TDs is subject to federal, state and local taxes. Let's assume the investor is subject to pay 25 percent federal taxes and 10 percent state taxes but no local taxes. How much does the investor earn on the Euro TD investment after taxes?

$$\text{Earnings After Taxes} = \$666.67 - (\$666.67 \times 25\%) - (\$666.67 \times 10\%)$$

Time Deposits of Financial Institutions

$$\text{Earnings After Taxes} = \$666.67 - \$166.67 - \$66.67$$

$$\text{Earnings After Taxes} = \$433.33$$

Now let's determine the investment's yield to maturity.

Formula

$$\text{Yield to Maturity} = \text{Rate of Interest}$$

Example

Yield to Maturity = 8%, or simply the Euro TD's stated rate of interest.

If we wanted to accurately compare this yield to that of a security quoted on a bond equivalent yield basis (like a Bill), we would have to convert one of the yields. In this example, let's convert the Euro TD's money market (or CD) equivalent yield into a bond equivalent yield.

Formula

$$\text{Bond Equivalent Yield} = \text{Money Market Yield} \times \frac{365}{360}$$

Example

$$\text{Bond Equivalent Yield} = 8\% \times \frac{365}{360}$$

$$\text{Bond Equivalent Yield} = .08111 = 8.11 \text{ percent}$$

Now let's determine cost and proceeds if an investor wishes to buy or sell a secondary CD (or Euro CD). The formulas to determine the cost and proceeds for buying and selling are identical. When selling a CD (or Euro CD), the investor receives a principal amount based on the face amount of the security and the price that the institution is willing to pay for the security. If the investor is purchasing, this principal (now based on face value and the price the institution is willing to sell at) must be paid. The price quoted by the institution will be expressed to the investor (whether selling or buying) as a yield percentage, such as 9 percent, 8.56 percent, or 7.78 percent. The investor must realize that this is a completely different percentage from the security's originally issued coupon rate. This "price yield," in fact, now becomes the security's yield to maturity. In addition, the seller receives from the purchaser the amount of interest that has accrued on the security from the time the security was issued (or the last coupon payment) until the day the transaction settles. The seller is entitled to this interest because the seller held the security during this time period. When the security matures (or at the next coupon payment) the new holder of the certificate will get all the interest. Since the purchaser then has received the interest he paid up front at the time of purchase, he really earns interest only for the period of time that he held the security.

The calculations to determine cost or proceeds for secondary deposits will take into account the security's original coupon, the original maturity, and the number of days to maturity as of the settlement date of the transaction. You may find the following formulas complex. Please, be patient and look over them carefully. Believe it or not, there is a logic to them. Besides, miraculous as it may seem, the formulas do work.

Time Deposits of Financial Institutions

Formula to Determine Cost or Proceeds of a Secondary Time Deposit

Step 1

$$\text{Price per \$1 of Face Value} = \frac{1 + \dfrac{\text{Original}}{\text{Coupon}} \times \left(\dfrac{\text{Original Issued}}{\text{Days to Maturity}} / 360\right)}{1 + \dfrac{\text{Yield}}{\text{Price}} \times \left(\dfrac{\text{Current Number of}}{\text{Days to Maturity}} / 360\right)}$$

Step 2

$$\text{Total Cost (or Proceeds)} = \text{Face Value} \times \text{Price Per \$1 of Face Value}$$

Now let's try an example using the formula. An investor is selling a CD. (Remember, this example and formulas could also be used for buying a secondary CD, buying a secondary Euro CD, or selling a secondary Euro CD.) The investor owns a $5,000,000 CD which has an original coupon of 9.75 percent and an original maturity of 120 days. The investor sells this CD at a yield price of 9.25 percent, with sixty days left to maturity at the time of settlement. How much will the investor receive from the sale?

Example

Step 1

$$\frac{\text{Price per \$1}}{\text{of Face Value}} = \frac{1 + 9.75\% \times (120/360)}{1 + 9.25\% \times (60/360)}$$

$$\frac{\text{Price per \$1}}{\text{of Face Value}} = \frac{1 + 9.75\% \times (.333)}{1 + 9.25\% \times (.167)}$$

$$\frac{\text{Price per \$1}}{\text{of Face Value}} = \frac{1 + .0324675}{1 + .0154475}$$

$$\text{Price Per \$1 of Face Value} = 1.016761$$

Step 2

$$\text{Total Proceeds} = \$5,000,000 \times 1.016761$$

$$\text{Total Proceeds} = \$5,083,805$$

OK, now we know how much the investor will receive from this sale. Let's carry this example one step further: let's determine how much of this total ($5,083,805) is made up of the security's principal (based on the price received) and how much is made up of the interest that was accrued until the time of sale. Here are the formulas needed to obtain these answers.

Formula to Determine Accrued Interest

$$\frac{\text{Accrued}}{\text{Interest}} = \frac{(\text{Face Value} \times \text{Original Coupon})}{360} \times \frac{\text{Number of Days Since}}{\text{Security Was Issued}}$$

Time Deposits of Financial Institutions

Formula to Determine How Much of the Total Was Due to Principal

$$\text{Principal} = \text{Total Cost} - \text{Accrued Interest}$$

Example

$$\frac{\text{Accrued}}{\text{Interest}} = \frac{(\$5,000,000 \times 9.75\%)}{(360)} \times 60$$

$$\text{Accrued Interest} = (\$1,354.17) \times 60$$

$$\text{Accrued Interest} = \$81,250.20$$

$$\text{Principal} = \$5,083,805 - \$81,250.20$$

$$\text{Principal} = \$5,002,554.80$$

Now you give it a shot! Determine the cost, interest earned if held to maturity, interest earned after taxes, and yield to maturity for the following purchase of a newly issued CD. The investor purchases a $175,000 CD, maturing in seventy-five days, at a rate of 8.15 percent. Assume a 28 percent federal and a 10 percent state tax rate.

COST

INTEREST EARNED IF HELD TO MATURITY

INTEREST EARNED AFTER TAXES

YIELD TO MATURITY

What would be this investment's bond equivalent yield to maturity?

Let's try an example using the purchase of a secondary Euro CD. The investor purchases a $1,000,000 Euro CD which has an original coupon of 8.60 percent, an original maturity of 180 days, and ninety-five days left until maturity as of the settlement date. It is

Time Deposits of Financial Institutions

being purchased at a yield price of 8.10 percent. How much will it cost the investor to purchase this Euro CD? Of the total cost, how much will be made up of the accrued interest that must be paid to the seller? How much of the total is the principal? If the investor holds this investment until maturity, how much interest will be received?

TOTAL COST

ACCRUED INTEREST

PRINCIPAL

INTEREST RECEIVED IF HELD UNTIL MATURITY

Chapter Five

BANKERS' ACCEPTANCES

A Bankers' Acceptance ("BA" for short) is another kind of bank obligation. There are two types of BAs: foreign BAs and domestic BAs. Domestic BAs are obligations of a U.S.-based bank. Foreign BAs are obligations of a U.S. agency or branch of a non-U.S.-based bank.

Typically, a BA's main purpose is to facilitate international trade. In international trade, exporters and importers often are not familiar with each other. In addition, country laws and customs of doing business can be different. If an exporter had to rely solely on the creditworthiness of a foreign importer for payment, he might feel wary about shipping goods. To add credibility to the promise that he will make the payment, the importer may ask his bank to formally commit to make the payment for the goods. Through this commitment, the exporter has obtained an added degree of safety. The payment will take place, even if the importer defaults. For this commitment, the bank will charge its customer, the importer, a fee and the importer will pay the bank for the committed funds on a specified date. This commitment is the BA.

A BA is in the form of a draft against the bank, specifying the amount and date of the bank's payment. Once the bank accepts this obligation, it stamps "Accepted" on the draft. Thus it has become a "Bankers' Acceptance." The "accepting" bank may wish to receive funds for the draft before the payment is due. To receive immediate funds, the bank may sell the draft as a security to investors. In order for the BA to become an attractive investment, the bank must sell it to investors below face value. So investors pay less than the face value at the time of purchase and receive the face value at maturity. Hence what is earned on the investment is the difference between the discount price paid for the BA and its face value. In other words, BAs are sold on a discount basis, similar to T-Bills and discount notes.

BAs are considered very safe investments. They usually are issued to mature in thirty to 180 days, and therefore, by the very nature of their short life span, are considered safe. But, more importantly, BAs are backed by the "accepting" institution. Investors can use whatever methods at their disposal to decide if they feel secure investing in a certain institution. BAs are also backed by the bank's customer, the importer who initiated the draft. The maker of the draft is obligated to make payment if the bank fails to do so. But, if the "accepting" institution becomes bankrupt, it is obligated to pay the investors holding its BAs first, even before its depositors. All these safety features enhance the popularity of BAs as an investment alternative.

Another appealing feature of BAs is their liquidity. BAs have one of the largest, most highly organized, and active secondary markets of all money market securities. The investor should have no trouble liquidating a BA before maturity. Similar to time deposits, the relative liquidity of a particular issuer's BAs is a function of the issuer's size, name recognition, and perceived creditworthiness. During the 1980's, the breadth of the foreign BA secondary market approached parity with that of the domestic BA market. This became especially true for Japanese bank BAs.

BAs are commonly issued in amounts of $500,000, $1,000,000 or $5,000,000, but can also be found in smaller or larger amounts as well. In fact, any size BA is possible. The determining factor is the specific amount stated on the draft. Some institutions will break up large size BAs and sell them to investors in smaller amounts (below the original face amount). Most institutions sell these "participations" to investors for no less than $100,000. Sometimes, though rarely, investors may find BAs for less than $100,000.

The interest earned on BAs is taxed the same way as time deposits. The interest is subject to the tax laws of the federal, state and local governments of the investor.

BAs are issued in a bearer, negotiable form, and therefore must be safekept. Similar to negotiable CDs, most BAs are safekept in New York. Investors may allow the institution they are purchasing the BA from to safekeep the security or may have the BAs delivered to their safe keeping agent in New York. The BA-selling institution usually will accommodate investors on this matter.

The yield level on BAs is affected by the overall level of short term interest rates in the marketplace. From this general rate level, BAs will always yield more than T-Bills and discount notes. Like time deposits, BAs are higher in yield because of the perception that government- and agency-backed securities are both safer and more liquid than securities backed by financial institutions. Therefore, a higher yield is offered to entice investors to purchase BAs.

The perceived creditworthiness of the particular issuer affects the yield on the issuer's BAs. The less creditworthy an institution is perceived in the marketplace, the higher its yield must be to entice investors. Foreign BAs tend to offer slightly higher yields than domestic BAs: the marketplace feels that BAs backed by U.S. banks are more secure than those backed by foreign banks. However, during the 1980's, the yield differential between foreign and domestic BAs narrowed significantly. In fact, in some cases today there is no difference in yield. Aside from credit quality, the yield received by the investor will be determined by the willingness of the institution to sell (or buy) the BA at market prices.

Most dealers sell more than one bank's BAs, which makes it easier for the investor to shop for the right BA. When buying a BA, the investor should tell the salesperson the desired accepting bank(s), the maturity date(s), and the face amount. Here's an example of how the salesperson may respond. "To meet your parameters, we can offer you a $500,000 Union Bank bankers' acceptance maturing on September 29, 1990 at a discount rate of 8.03 percent. When selling a BA, the investor must tell the salesperson the accepting bank, the maturity date, the face value, and the preferred settlement date. If the price quoted by the institution is acceptable to the investor, the transaction is completed. Settlement date, funds transfer, and security transfer are discussed and agreed to by the buyer and the seller. At maturity, the BAs will be presented to the issuer for payment of the face value and the investor will receive these funds in the manner determined at the time of sale.

Let's go through an example to determine the cost, interest earned, amount received at maturity, and yield to maturity on the purchase of a BA. In this example, the investor purchases a $1,000,000 BA, to mature ninety days from the settlement date, at a discount rate of 8.10 percent. You will notice that because BAs are quoted on a discount basis, the cost is calculated using the same formula that is used for bills and discount notes. While the yield on bills and discount notes are quoted on a bond equivalent basis, the yield on BAs are quoted on a money market (or CD) equivalent basis. Therefore, the formula to determine a BA's yield to maturity is different from that used for bills and discount notes: it assumes a 360-day year.

Formula to Determine the Cost of a BA

$$\frac{\text{Discount Amount}}{} = \frac{(\text{Face Value} \times \text{Discount Rate})}{360} \times \text{Number of Days to maturity}$$

$$\text{Cost of a BA} = \text{Face Amount} - \text{Discount Amount}$$

Example

$$\frac{\text{Discount Amount}}{} = \frac{(\$1,000,000 \times 8.10\%)}{360} \times 90$$

$$\frac{\text{Discount Amount}}{} = \frac{(\$81,000)}{360} \times 90$$

$$\text{Discount Amount} = \$20,250$$

$$\text{Cost} = \$1{,}000{,}000 - \$20{,}250$$

$$\text{Cost} = \$979{,}750$$

Formula to Determine Interest Earned at Maturity

$$\text{Interest Earned} = \text{Discount Amount}$$

Example

Interest Earned = $20,250, or the difference between what the investor pays for the BA, $979,750, and what the investor receives at maturity, $1,000,000 (the face value).

Assuming that the investor is subject to a 25 percent federal and a 10 percent state income tax rate, how much will he earn?

Formula

$$\text{After-Tax Earnings} = \text{Total Interest Earned} - \left(\text{Total Interest Earned} \times \text{Tax Rate}\right)$$

Example

$$\text{After-Tax Earnings} = \$20{,}250 - (\$20{,}250 \times 25\%) - (\$20{,}250 \times 10\%)$$

$$\text{After-Tax Earnings} = \$20{,}250 - (\$5062.50) - (\$2{,}025)$$

$$\text{After-Tax Earnings} = \$13{,}162.50$$

Formula to Determine CD Equivalent Yield to Maturity

$$\frac{\text{Yield to}}{\text{Maturity}} = \frac{\text{Discount}}{(\text{Face Amount} - \text{Discount})} \times \frac{360}{\text{Days to Maturity}}$$

Example

$$\frac{\text{Yield to}}{\text{Maturity}} = \frac{\$20{,}250}{(\$1{,}000{,}000 - \$20{,}250)} \times \frac{360}{90}$$

$$\frac{\text{Yield to}}{\text{Maturity}} = \frac{\$20{,}250}{\$979{,}750} \times \frac{360}{90}$$

Yield to Maturity = .082674 = 8.27 percent

Now let's convert this CD equivalent yield into a bond equivalent yield. This will enable us to compare the yield on a BA to the yield on securities that are computed assuming a 365 day year.

Formula to Convert a CD Equivalent Yield into a Bond Equivalent

$$\frac{\text{Bond Equivalent}}{\text{Yield}} = \frac{\text{CD Equivalent}}{\text{Yield}} \times \frac{365}{360}$$

Example

$$\frac{\text{Bond Equivalent}}{\text{Yield}} = 8.27\% \times \frac{365}{360}$$

Bond Equivalent Yield = .0838486 = 8.39 percent

Using the same example, let's say the investor decides to sell the BA sixty days from maturity. The investor receives an 8.20 percent bid rate from a financial institution, which is accepted. How much money is received from the sale? How much was earned from the investment? We can use the same formula to determine the proceeds from the sale of a BA as we used to determine the cost of the purchase.

Formula

$$\frac{\text{Discount Amount}}{} = \frac{(\text{Face Value} \times \text{Discount Rate})}{360} \times \text{Number of Days to maturity}$$

$$\text{Proceeds From the Sale} = \text{Face Amount} - \text{Discount Amount}$$

Example

$$\frac{\text{Discount Amount}}{} = \frac{(\$1{,}000{,}000 \times 8.20\%)}{360} \times 60$$

$$\frac{\text{Discount Amount}}{} = \frac{(\$82{,}000)}{360} \times 60$$

$$\text{Discount Amount} = \$13{,}666.67$$

$$\text{Proceeds From the Sale} = \$1{,}000{,}000 - \$13{,}666.67$$

$$\text{Proceeds From the Sale} = \$986{,}333.33$$

To determine how much was earned from the sale, subtract the cost of the original purchase from the proceeds of the sale.

Formula

$$\text{Amount Earned From the Investment} = \text{Proceeds of Sale} - \text{Cost of Purchase}$$

Example

$$\text{Amount Earned From the Investment} = \$986{,}333.33 - \$979{,}750$$

$$\text{Amount Earned From the Investment} = \$6{,}583.33$$

The investor should realize that two factors went into producing $6,583.33 in earnings. First, the investor held the BA for thirty days, thus earning interest for that time period. The market value of the BA depreciated from an 8.10 percent discount at the time of purchase to an 8.20 percent discount at the time of sale.

Once again it is your turn to go through these steps. Given the following example, determine a BA's purchase cost, interest earned if held to maturity, earnings after taxes, and both the CD and bond equivalent yields to maturity.

The investor purchases a $5,000,000 BA which matures in 120 days, at a discount rate of 7.99 percent. We will assume the investor is in the 26 percent federal and 11 percent state income tax brackets. The answers, along with explanations, are in Appendix A.

COST

INTEREST EARNED AT MATURITY

Bankers' Acceptances

EARNINGS AFTER TAXES

CD EQUIVALENT YIELD TO MATURITY

BOND EQUIVALENT YIELD TO MATURITY

The investor decides to sell the BA with seventy-three days left to maturity. The selling rate received is 8.12 percent. What are the proceeds from the sale and the earnings from the investment?

PROCEEDS

EARNINGS

Chapter Six

COMMERCIAL PAPER

Commercial paper is a short-term, unsecured obligation issued by both financial companies and non-financial companies to help satisfy their short-term funding needs. Commercial paper may be issued by U.S. or foreign companies. Typically, commercial paper is issued by large corporations that have received the highest credit ratings available. Commercial paper is one of the most popular money market securities because it is usually backed by large, highly rated companies and offers all of the following: competitive yields, an option in the payment of interest, an option in the form of ownership, short maturities, liquidity, and low minimum denominations.

Commercial paper can be obtained in one of two ways. Issuers set their rates for various maturities based on their specific needs. Some issuers have their own sales staff to sell their securities to investors. In that case, the investor can buy directly from the issuer. Other issuers sell through commercial paper dealer(s). These issuers quote their rates directly to the dealer(s), and then the dealer's salespeople quote the rates to investors and distribute the commercial paper. In either case, the funds are being invested in the issuer's commercial paper, to mature on a stated date, at the rate offered by the issuer for that maturity.

Commercial paper is considered a very safe investment. First, similar to the other securities in this book, it is considered safe by the nature of its short life span. There is very little perceived risk of a highly rated company going bankrupt during the typically short life of a commercial paper investment. Commercial paper is backed solely by the issuer. The issuers are all analyzed by the credit rating agencies which we've discussed. By reviewing the company's reputation, financial history, and credit ratings, the investor can decide whether or not to invest. In fact, the vast majority of commercial paper is issued by companies that have the highest credit ratings given by these agencies. For further safety, issuers frequently back the commercial paper with a bank(s) line of credit. This insures that if the issuer has difficulty paying off their short-term debt, the bank will provide funds.

Commercial paper can be issued for a minimum of $25,000 but usually is issued for a minimum of $100,000. The issuer decides the minimum denomination and the incremental amount over the minimum that they will accept. Most issuers allow any incremental amount over the stated minimum.

Commercial paper can be issued to mature from one to 270 days. Keeping commercial paper to a maximum maturity of 270 days allows the issuer to avoid the Securities and Exchange Commission's (SEC) registration requirements, which can be both costly and time-consuming for the issuer. Many investors take advantage of the ability to invest in commercial paper for only one day, an alternative to Euro TDs and repurchase agreements (which we will learn about in Chapter Seven). The most actively purchased maturities are one to forty-five days.

An investor may liquidate commercial paper before maturity, however the secondary market for commercial paper is not as active as those for the other securities discussed thus far. Historically, a very small percentage of commercial paper is liquidated before maturity. Many issuers, upon request from the investor, will buy back their own commercial paper. The investor can also liquidate by selling the commercial paper to a commercial paper dealer. Because the secondary market for commercial paper is not as active as other short-term securities, and because issuers prefer not to buy back their paper, the prices received when selling may not always be favorable.

Taxes affect the interest earned on commercial paper in the same way as interest on time deposits, BAs, and some discount notes. The interest earned is subject to how the federal, state, and local income tax laws pertain to the investor.

A popular characteristic of commercial paper is the way interest is paid to the investor. With commercial paper, the investor has the choice of having interest paid at maturity or purchasing the security on a discount basis. Either way the rate offered to the investor is the same. For example, let's say General Motors quotes its thirty-day commercial paper at 8 percent. Now let's say the investor chooses to purchase $100,000 of the security with interest received at maturity. The investor will pay $100,000 for the purchase and receive interest on this principal, based on 8 percent for thirty days. There is, however, a slight variation in the way interest is computed for interest-bearing commercial paper as compared to the other interest-bearing securities discussed. The formula to determine interest is different because all rates for commercial paper are quoted on a discount basis. We will learn how this variation affects both interest and yield calculations later in this chapter.

If, on the other hand, the investor chooses the discount method, the purchase cost is based on a discount rate of 8 percent for thirty days. The interest is the difference between the discount cost and the $100,000, identical to the other discounted securities discussed. Choosing between the two methods is strictly based on the preference of the investor. For the identical investment, if the investor chooses the discount method both the cost and the interest earned will be less than if he had chosen the interest bearing method.

The investor also has the choice of having the securities issued in book-entry or bearer form. If the investor opts for book-entry form, a computer entry identifies the transaction and the investor receives only a confirmation statement as proof of ownership. Many issuers require a commercial paper purchase of at least $1 million before they will issue a bearer certificate. Many large investors opt for this form when buying. Once again, because this is a negotiable instrument, it requires safekeeping. Because commercial paper issuers have investors all over the country, they too issue their certificates in New York. The investor's New York safekeeping custodian can thus take possession of the certificates upon purchase and present the certificate to the issuer's New York agent for payment at maturity.

The factors that determine the rates offered by commercial paper issuers are similar to those affecting yields on other types of short-term debt. The general level of short-term rates is the primary factor influencing commercial paper rates. If, for example, all short-term debt obligations in the marketplace are yielding between 8 percent and 9 percent, most commercial paper will yield within or near this range.

The next factor is investors' perception of the risk of commercial paper compared to other short-term securities. Commercial paper always yields higher than T-Bills and discount notes. Once again, a government or agency guarantee is perceived as safer than a corporate guarantee. Furthermore, bills and discount notes are more liquid than commercial paper. Therefore it makes sense that to attract investors away from government issues, commercial paper must yield more.

The relationship between yields on commercial paper and yields on bank obligations varies over time and is a function of the supply of and the demand for these securities. Affecting the demand side of this equation is investors' perception of the risk of corporate versus bank debt obligations, at any one time. On the supply side, if commercial paper issuers in general are seeking more funds relative to other borrowers, commercial paper rates will be higher than rates on comparable securities to attract investors.

Another factor affecting the rates offered by a commercial paper issuer is the supply of, and the demand for, that particular issuer's commercial paper. An issuer's expectation for the direction of interest rates in general may influence how competitively that issuer prices a specific maturity sector. If, for example, an issuer feels that rates will drop soon, it may offer more competitive rates on shorter maturities to attract short-term funds. If these expectations prove correct, when these securities mature the issuer can reissue at lower rates. An issuer facing a particularly strong need for funds may offer rates higher than its rival issuers for the maturities sought. On

Commercial Paper

the investor demand side of this equation, if an issuer is perceived to have a lower credit standing than their rival issuers, there will be less demand for its paper and it will have to offer higher rates than its rivals to attract investors.

Now the investor has decided to purchase commercial paper. Investors typically go to commercial paper dealers for quotes on several issuers' paper. This gives the investor the opportunity to see which of their favorite issuers is offering the highest rate for the desired maturity. The investor should tell the dealer the amount of money he wants to invest, for what maturity, and from which issuer(s). The salesperson then tells the investor the rates of the specified issuers, which paper his firm is authorized to sell, and which meet the investor's parameters. For example, let's say the investor wishes to invest $100,000 for thirty days and is undecided about the issuer. The dealer may quote rates such as General Motors at 8 percent, General Electric at 8.05 percent, and American Express at 8.10 percent. The investor tells the salesperson which paper he wants. At this time, the investor and dealer agree on how funds and securities will be transferred and on the settlement date. Most commercial paper transactions are done for same day (cash) settlement.

Here's an example how to determine the purchase cost, interest earned at maturity, and yield to maturity when an investor purchases newly issued commercial paper. We will determine these figures under the two methods that commercial paper can be purchased: interest-bearing or discounted. In this example, the investor wishes to purchase $110,000 of commercial paper to mature in forty-five days at a rate of 9.10 percent. We will first go through the example as if the investor purchased the commercial paper on a discount basis.

Formula to Determine the Cost of Discounted Commercial Paper

$$\frac{\text{Discount}}{\text{Amount}} = \frac{(\text{Face Value} \times \text{Discount Rate})}{360} \times \frac{\text{Number of Days}}{\text{to Maturity}}$$

$$\text{Cost} = \text{Face Value} - \text{Discount Amount}$$

Example

$$\frac{\text{Discount}}{\text{Amount}} = \frac{(\$110{,}000 \times 9.10\%)}{360} \times 45$$

$$\frac{\text{Discount}}{\text{Amount}} = \frac{(\$110{,}000 \times .091)}{360} \times 45$$

$$\frac{\text{Discount}}{\text{Amount}} = \frac{\$10{,}010}{360} \times 45$$

$$\text{Discount Amount} = \$1{,}251.25$$

$$\text{Cost} = \$110{,}000 - \$1{,}251.25$$

$$\text{Cost} = \$108{,}748.75$$

Formula to Determine Interest Earned on Discounted Commercial Paper

$$\text{Interest Earned} = \text{Discounted Amount}$$

Example

$$\text{Interest Earned} = \$1{,}251.25$$

At maturity, the investor receives the security's face value, in this case $110,000.

Do not forget, the interest earned on commercial paper is subject to federal, state, and local tax rules and rates. Let's assume that the investor must pay federal and state taxes on the commercial paper earnings based on 25 percent federal and 10 percent state rates.

After taxes, how much will the investor retain?

$$\text{After-Tax Earnings} = \$1{,}251.25 - (\$1{,}251.25 \times 25\%) - (\$1{,}251.25 \times 10\%)$$

After-Tax Earnings = $1,251.25 − ($312.81) − ($125.13)

After-Tax Earnings = $813.31

Formula for Yield to Maturity on Discounted Commercial Paper

$$\text{Yield to Maturity} = \frac{\text{Discount}}{\text{Face Amount} - \text{Discount}} \times \frac{360}{\text{Days to Maturity}}$$

Example

$$\text{Yield to Maturity} = \frac{\$1,251.25}{\$110,000 - \$1,251.25} \times \frac{360}{45}$$

$$\text{Yield to Maturity} = \frac{\$1,251.25}{\$108,748.75} \times \frac{360}{45}$$

Yield to Maturity = .0920464 = 9.20 percent

The yield to maturity for commercial paper is quoted on a money market (or CD) equivalent basis. Let's now convert this figure to a bond equivalent yield.

Formula to Convert From a CD to a Bond Equivalent Yield

$$\text{Bond Equivalent} = \text{CD Equivalent} \times \frac{365}{360}$$

$$\text{Bond Equivalent} = 9.20\% \times \frac{365}{360}$$

Bond Equivalent Yield to Maturity = .0932777 = 9.33 percent

Now, using the same example, let's assume the investor purchased the commercial paper on an interest bearing basis. Remember, rates on interest-bearing commercial paper are also quoted on a discount basis, so different formulas are used to determine the amount of interest earned and the yield to maturity for interest-bearing commercial paper than for other interest-bearing securities. To refresh your memory, the investor is purchasing commercial paper for $110,000 at a rate of 9.10 percent for forty-five days. Let's determine cost, interest earned, and yield to maturity.

Formula to Determine Cost of Interest-Bearing Commercial Paper

$$\text{Cost} = \text{Face Value}$$

Example

$$\text{Cost} = \$110{,}000$$

Formula for Interest Earned on Interest-Bearing Commercial Paper

$$\frac{\text{Interest}}{\text{Earned}} = \frac{(\text{Rate} \times \text{Face} \times \text{Number of Days to Maturity}/360)}{\text{Face} - (\text{Rate} \times \text{Face} \times \text{Number of Days to Maturity}/360)} \times \text{Face}$$

Example

$$\frac{\text{Interest}}{\text{Earned}} = \frac{(9.10\% \times \$110{,}000 \times 45/360)}{\$110{,}000 - (9.10\% \times \$110{,}000 \times 45/360)} \times \$110{,}000$$

$$\frac{\text{Interest}}{\text{Earned}} = \frac{(.091 \times \$110{,}000 \times 45/360)}{\$110{,}000 - (.091 \times \$110{,}000 \times 45/360)} \times \$110{,}000$$

$$\frac{\text{Interest}}{\text{Earned}} = \frac{\$1{,}251.25}{\$110{,}000 - \$1{,}251.25} \times \$110{,}000$$

$$\frac{\text{Interest}}{\text{Earned}} = \frac{\$1{,}251.25}{\$108{,}748.75} \times \$110{,}000$$

$$\text{Interest Earned} = .0115058 \times \$110{,}000$$

$$\text{Interest Earned} = \$1{,}265.64$$

At maturity, the investor receives principal plus interest, or: $110,000 + $1,265.64 = $111,265.64.

Remember, the investor is in the 25 percent federal and 10 percent state income tax brackets. How much will the investor retain after taxes?

$$\text{After-Tax Earnings} = \$1{,}265.64 - (\$1{,}265.64 \times 25\%) - (\$1{,}265.64 \times 10\%)$$

$$\text{After-Tax Earnings} = \$1{,}265.64 - \$316.41 - \$126.56$$

$$\text{After-Tax Earnings} = \$822.67$$

Formula to Determine Yield to Maturity

$$\frac{\text{Yield to}}{\text{Maturity}} = \frac{\text{Discount}}{\text{Face Value}} \times \frac{360}{\text{Days to Maturity}}$$

Example

$$\frac{\text{Yield to}}{\text{Maturity}} = \frac{\$1{,}265.64}{\$110{,}000} \times \frac{360}{45}$$

$$\text{Yield To Maturity} = .0115058 \times 360 / 45$$

$$\text{Yield To Maturity} = .0920464 = 9.20 \text{ percent}$$

Some commercial paper issuers assume a 365 day year. In this case, the investor needs to substitute 365 for 360 in the above formulas.

If it is desired to convert this yield to a bond equivalent yield, the investor uses the same formula that is used to convert discounted commercial paper. In this example, since both the discounted and interest-bearing commercial paper yields 9.20 percent, the bond equivalent yields for both will be 9.33 percent.

Now here is an example for you. An investor purchases $250,00 of commercial paper to mature in thirty days at a rate of 8.55 percent. Assume the investor is subject to 26 percent federal and 11 percent state income tax rates. How much will the investment cost? How much will be earned in interest? How much will be retained after taxes? How much will be received at maturity? And, what are the CD and bond equivalent yields to maturity? Make these calculations for both the discounted and interest-bearing methods of buying commercial paper.

Purchasing the Commercial Paper on a Discount Basis

COST

INTEREST EARNED

TOTAL RECEIVED AT MATURITY

Commercial Paper 103

EARNINGS AFTER TAXES

CD YIELD TO MATURITY

BOND EQUIVALENT YIELD TO MATURITY

Purchasing the Commercial Paper on Interest-Bearing Basis

COST

INTEREST EARNED

TOTAL RECEIVED AT MATURITY

EARNINGS AFTER TAXES

CD YIELD TO MATURITY

BOND EQUIVALENT YIELD TO MATURITY

Chapter Seven

REPURCHASE AGREEMENTS

A Repurchase Agreement (commonly known as a "Repo" or "RP") is a deposit with a stated maturity and interest rate at a financial institution. At maturity, the institution promises to pay the investor the principal deposited along with earned interest for the period of the deposit.

This, however, is a very simple definition of a repurchase agreement. There is in fact more to a repo. Repos originate because financial institutions have a need to fund their operations and security holdings. As a way to attract funds, the institution will issue a deposit (the repo) which is backed (collateralized) by securities the institution owns. This collateral gives the investor added protection, while allowing the institution to typically assign a lower rate on the deposit than their usual method of attracting short-term funds, Federal Funds, which are uncollateralized. Federal Funds (Fed Funds) are excess reserve balances which banks lend to each other typically on a short-term basis.

Technically, when a repurchase agreement is transacted, the investor purchases one of the securities owned by the institution. The investor may specify the type of collateral desired for purchase. The institution may or may not possess the securities desired by the investor. Assuming that the investor approves of the collateral, the investor purchases the securities, or deposits his funds with the

107

institution. The institution agrees to buy back those same securities on an agreed upon date, at the same price originally used to sell to the investor, in essence returning the investor's principal deposit. Leaving his funds with the institution, the investor earns the stated rate of return on the principal. Thus comes the name, "repurchase agreement." From the institution's point of view, the selling of their securities with the promise to buy back is referred to as a Reverse Repurchase Agreement.

Very little risk exists with RPs. They are guaranteed by the borrowing institution (which is holding the deposit). But more important, the securities used in a RP transaction are collateral on the deposit, thus making the RP a secured loan. Should the institution fail to buy back the securities, or in essence fail to return principal and interest, the investor has possession of the securities and could sell them to recover his principal. The majority of RPs are collateralized by U.S. government and or agency securities. As we know, these are the safest and most liquid securities available, so selling them to recover the invested funds would not be a problem. And, the collateral's value at the time of purchase usually exceeds the deposit amount to cushion the impact of any depreciation of the securities during the term of the RP.

Some RPs are collateralized by other types of securities. The advantage to investors of using non-government securities as collateral is a higher rate of return. In fact, investors may specify the type of collateral they wish to have backing their deposit. Investors typically allow the same securities for collateral as they would purchase outright.

Typically, the minimum amount required for a repo is $100,000. However, the minimum denomination varies from institution to institution. Some have been known to accept RPs for less than $100,000. Institutions typically accept any incremental amount over the stated minimum.

Theoretically, RPs can be outstanding for any length of time agreed to by the buyer and the seller. This makes them appealing to those who wish to have their funds invested until a specific date. Most RPs mature in one to thirty days. In fact, the vast majority of RPs are bought to mature the next business day and are rolled over as needed. RPs are a popular alternative to commercial paper and

Euro TDs as a one-day investment. Some repos are bought on a "continuing contract" or "open maturity" basis, which means there is no stated maturity. An investor purchases a series of "next business day" RPs and each business day a new interest rate is set for the deposit by the institution, based on current market conditions. The transaction may be terminated at any time, by either party. This type of RP appeals to some investors as a means of reducing transaction costs since a new transaction and transfer of funds every day is not needed.

Although no secondary market exists for RPs, they are considered a liquid investment. Remember, the vast majority of RPs mature on the next business day. Thus, investors have the option of keeping their funds and not reinvesting. This also holds true with "open contract" repos: if the investor needs the funds he can discontinue the repo and receive his funds on the same business day. If the institution defaults on the RP, the investor can sell the securities that are serving as collateral to receive immediate cash since the securities held by the investor typically are ones with large secondary markets. Finally, if the investor owns a term RP (maturing in more than one day) and wants to liquidate before maturity, he can negotiate the early liquidation with the borrowing institution. Often the institution will accommodate the investor by buying back the securities (thus terminating the RP) before the agreed-to maturity date. As you can see, the repo investor has several avenues to receive funds on short notice.

Taxation effects and the payment of interest earned on a repo are similar to many of the other securities already discussed. The interest earned from a repo is subject to taxation by the investor's federal, state, and local governments. Interest on RPs is paid at the time of maturity. Interest is calculated as a percentage of principal deposit for the number of days the RP was outstanding. For example, let's say an investor purchases a $100,000 RP to mature in one day at a rate of 8 percent. The investor pays $100,000 and receives the next day $100,000 plus 8 percent interest for one day on the $100,000.

RPs are most commonly transacted in book-entry form. In most cases, the institution involved in the RP transaction safekeeps the securities (collateral) that the investor has purchased, although the investor has been assigned that specific security. The institution either receives a funds wire, or reduces the investor's account at the institution to receive payment for the RP. The investor receives a confirmation statement presenting the terms of the repo and a description of the collateral.

In some cases, the investor may request to take possession of the securities used as collateral. This is typically done with large investors who do not safekeep securities with the RP transacting institution. In this case, the institution delivers the securities to the investor's safekeeping agent and the investor has funds wired to the RP-selling institution. At maturity, the investor's safekeeping agent sends the securities back to the institution and the investor receives principal plus interest.

RPs generally are priced below the Federal Funds rate (the rate of interest charged by banks when lending their excess reserves to other banks on a short-term basis) because RPs are secured loans (backed by securities serving as collateral) while Federal Funds are not secured. Federal Funds are only guaranteed by the creditworthiness of the institution. Because RPs are considered safer, they can offer a lower return. RPs backed by U.S. government or agency securities typically offer a lower return than RPs backed by bank or corporate issued securities because they are considered riskier.

The rates offered on RPs are also influenced by the daily supply and demand of funds and collateral in the marketplace. The more securities that institutions possess that need to be funded, the more upward pressure on RP rates. Institutions must offer higher rates to attract investors away from alternatives. Of course, a specific institution's supply of collateral and need for funds directly influence how competitively the institution will price its RPs. Obviously, if the institution has a particularly large supply of collateral, and a large funding need, it may offer a slightly higher RP rate than its competitors. Investor demand for short-term securities also influences RP rates. For example, the higher the demand for very short securities throughout the marketplace will put downward pressure on RP rates. This tends to happen before tax payment periods or when investors feel that interest rates will be moving higher soon.

Once the investor has decided to purchase a repo he must tell the salesperson the amount of the investment and the desired maturity.

Repurchase Agreements

At this time, the investor should also tell the salesperson if they wish to have a different institution take possession of the collateral, and what type of securities are desired for collateral. If the institution has the securities to satisfy the investor's needs, the salesperson will state the rate offered for the RP. If this rate is acceptable to the investor, the transaction takes place. The two parties will agree on how funds will be transferred and the settlement date. Most RPs settle on the day of the transaction, however settlement can occur on whatever date is agreed on. Also at this time the investor can find out from the salesperson what specific securities are involved in the RP. For example, the investor may request to purchase a $100,000 RP to mature in three days backed by U.S. Treasury securities. If the institution is able to accommodate the investor, the salesperson may say something like, "We can offer a rate of 8 percent on the RP. The collateral for the RP will be $105,000 U.S. Treasury Bills maturing on February 17, 1991."

Now let's go through an example to determine the cost, interest earned, and yield to maturity on a repurchase agreement. An investor purchases a $175,000 RP to mature in five days at a rate of 8.25 percent. The yield to maturity on a repo is quoted on a CD equivalent basis. RPs are most commonly compared to other money market securities, such as commercial paper and Euro TDs, whose yields are also calculated on a CD basis. Thus, rarely will the investor need to convert a repo's yield to a bond equivalent yield, and so we will not go through this exercise for RPs.

Formula to Determine the Cost of an RP

$$\text{Cost} = \text{Face Value}$$

Example

$$\text{Cost} = \$175,000$$

Formula to Determine the Interest Earned on an RP

$$\frac{\text{Interest}}{\text{Earned}} = \frac{(\text{Face Value} \times \text{Rate})}{360} \times \frac{\text{Number of Days}}{\text{to Maturity}}$$

Example

$$\frac{\text{Interest}}{\text{Earned}} = \frac{(\$175{,}000 \times 8.25\%)}{360} \times 5$$

$$\frac{\text{Interest}}{\text{Earned}} = \frac{(\$14{,}437.50)}{360} \times 5$$

$$\text{Interest Earned} = \$200.52$$

Assuming the investor must pay 28 percent federal and 12 percent state income taxes on these earnings, how much is retained after taxes?

$$\text{After-Tax Earnings} = \$200.52 - (\$200.52 \times 28\%) - (\$200.52 \times 12\%)$$

$$\text{After-Tax Earnings} = \$200.52 - \$56.15 - \$24.06$$

$$\text{After-Tax Earnings} = \$120.31$$

Formula for Yield to Maturity

$$\text{Yield to Maturity} = \text{Rate}$$

Example

$$\text{Yield to Maturity} = 8.25 \text{ percent}$$

Repurchase Agreements

Now you go through a similar exercise. An investor purchases a $100,000 RP to mature in three days at a rate of 8.10 percent. Calculate the cost, interest earned, interest earned after taxes (assume the investor must pay 26 percent federal and 11 percent state income taxes on the earnings), and yield to maturity for this investment.

COST

INTEREST EARNED

INTEREST EARNED AFTER TAXES

Chapter 7

YIELD TO MATURITY

Chapter Eight

CASE STUDY

This book has discussed the most popular money market securities. Now we must take the next step in the learning process: determining which of these securities to invest in. A case study is used in this chapter to help explain the process of identifying the "best" short-term investment. The reader must realize that there is no universally best investment. What is the optimal security for one investor may not be for another investor. Also, what might be the best security for an investor today may not be tomorrow. The determination is based on the investor's limitations, goals, biases and the marketplace. What the reader should try to obtain from this section is an understanding of what every investor should think about before investing. We will go through a case study of a specific investor, determining which money market security is best given his particular circumstances. Then you will be asked to determine the best security for an investor with a completely different set of circumstances.

As a reference to help with these cases and future investment decisions, Appendices B, C, and D have been set up to help summarize and organize the information in the previous chapters. In Appendix B, the reader will find each security along with a summary of each of their most important characteristics. For example, let's say the reader wanted a quick summary of T-Bills. He would just have to turn to page 149 of the Appendix to find the summary on T-Bills. For each security, the reader will find the following characteristics: guarantor, denominations, increments, original maturities, tax effects, type of interest payments, and available forms of ownership.

Appendix C highlights each important characteristic of a money market security. Each security is placed into the appropriate category within the characteristic. For example, let's say the reader wanted a quick summary of who guarantees each security. The reader need only turn to page 159 of Appendix C to find this information. The reader will find on this page that the U.S. Government guarantees T-Bills, financial institutions guarantee CDs, etc. The characteristics listed are: guarantor, most common minimum denomination, earliest original maturity, longest original maturity, tax effects, available forms of ownership, and type of interest payments available.

Appendix D takes every two combinations of characteristics from Appendix C and places one on the horizontal axis and the other on the vertical axis to form a matrix. This allows the reader to see how each security compares under two characteristics. For example, let's say the reader wanted to know what securities are guaranteed by an agency of the federal government and are available for $25,000. The reader need only to turn to page 168 to find "Guarantor" and "Minimum Denomination" on opposite axes. The reader should look at the "Agency of U.S. Gov't" column under "Guarantor" and the "$25,000" row under "Minimum Denomination" to determine the answer. Doing this he will observe that FHLMC, FNMA and FFCB Discount Notes are both guaranteed by an agency of the federal government and available for $25,000. The potential investor should find these appendices most helpful in making the investment decision.

Now for the case study, featuring investor Max Massey.

MAX MASSEY

Max Massey has $50,000 he wants to invest for less than one year. Max has determined that one year from now he will need the money for the downpayment on a new car and for furniture. Max considers himself a conservative investor. He feels most comfortable investing in securities backed by the U.S. government or its agencies. Max also wants to invest in a security which is highly liquid. He does not expect to need the money before the end of the year, but he wants to be certain he can quickly convert his securities to cash if an unexpected need arises. Max really does not care what form the securities are in, nor how interest will be paid. Max expects that sometime during the middle of the year interest rates will rise. Max would like to time his investment to take advantage of this expected movement, thus maximizing his total return for the year. Max must pay taxes on the earnings of investments, based on his 27 percent federal and 11 percent state income tax brackets. Which money market security best fits Max's needs based on his limitations, goals and biases?

First, Max is limited by the amount of money he has to invest--$50,000. Second, he has narrowed his choices to those securities backed by the U.S. government and its agencies. Max could quickly narrow the field by looking at the matrix with the headings Minimum Denomination and Guarantor (Appendix D, page 168). Max should look at the columns marked U.S. Government and U.S. Government Agency, on the Guarantor axis, then at the rows marked $25,000, $10,000, and $5,000 on the Minimum Denomination axis. Max can consider the securities that fall into these six boxes. Looking at these boxes, Max finds that he can choose between T-Bills, FFCB discount notes, FNMA discount notes and FHLMC discount notes.

Max expects rates to rise within the next six months, so he may want to invest now in a security maturing in six months rather than twelve months. If rates do rise in the next six months, Max can reinvest his money for the remaining six months at higher rates than those available now. Thus Max will earn more and still stay within his desired one year maximum maturity. Max should now look at the lists presenting the maturity ranges (Appendix C, pages 161-162) and see that the four securities all have six-month maturities. Thus, all are still in contention.

Since all four securities meet his criteria, Max may now base his decision on which of the four offers the highest return. Upon calling his financial institution, Max is given the following price and yield quotes on the four securities, assuming $50,000 and a six-month maturity:

Security	Discount Rate Price (%)	Bond Equivalent Yield (%)
T-Bill	8.20	8.70
FHLMC Discount Note	8.55	9.05
FNMA Discount Note	8.50	9.00
FFCB Discount Note	8.45	8.95

Based on the quotes obtained, it appears that FHLMC discount notes, at 9.05 percent, offer the highest return. But, let's not forget that these yields are based on pre-tax earnings. Since the earnings on all four securities are subject to federal taxation, Max can ignore this as a means for comparison. Now, Max should turn to the list that shows which securities are subject to state taxation (Appendix C, page 163). This list shows that of these four securities, FHLMC and FNMA discount notes produce earnings which are subject to state taxation. Therefore, their yields must be adjusted to account for the state taxation. After all, a portion of the earnings will not be retained by Max but must be relinquished to his state. Since FHLMC discount notes offer a higher yield than FNMA's, Max will eliminate the FNMA notes from consideration and only adjust the FHLMC's yield to compare with the state-tax-free securities. Max is in the 11 percent state income tax bracket so 89 percent (100 percent − 11 percent) will be retained by Max. Therefore, the FHLMC discount note's after-state-tax yield is:

$$9.06 \text{ percent} \times 89 \text{ percent} = 8.06 \text{ percent}$$

Now that Max has adjusted the yield for state taxes, he sees that FFCB discount notes offer the highest yield at 8.95 percent. Remember, Max does not have to pay state tax on the earnings of FFCB discount notes. So, Max decides to invest his $50,000 in a FFCB discount note, maturing in six months. This security satisfies all his requirements. FFCB discount notes are:

1. Backed by an agency of the federal government
2. Obtainable for $50,000
3. Liquid
4. Available in a six-month maturity
5. Highest yielding among acceptable securities, based on his state tax bracket

Now it is your turn. Based on the following description, determine the optimal money market investment for Bradley Morris.

BRADLEY MORRIS

Bradley Morris is the assistant treasurer of KJB Studios. He has determined that his company has $1,000,000 that will not be needed for three months. The company's normal cash flow should cover expenses until then. In three months, KJB will need the funds to pay for new equipment. Bradley has decided to invest all of the $1,000,000 for the entire three-month period. And, he does not want his investment to mature before the money is needed because he believes that interest rates will not move significantly during this period and because he wants to avoid reinvesting his principal. Bradley has been instructed by his superiors to invest in securities backed by the highest-rated U.S.-based companies, the largest local bank (First National Bank), the U.S. government, or a government agency. Bradley is certain that the funds will not be needed for three months, but just in case he is wrong he wants the funds invested in a relatively liquid security. KJB Studios is headquartered in a state that does not tax the earnings on securities owned by companies. Bradley is indifferent about the form of ownership and the form of interest payment. Based on these parameters and the offering prices of the following three-month securities, which security do you recommend for Bradley?

Security	Price Quote (%)	CD Yield (%)
T-Bill	7.70	7.86
FFCB Discount Note	7.80	7.96
FNMA Discount Note	7.90	8.06
FHLMC Discount Note	7.88	8.04
FHLB Discount Note	7.83	7.99
First National Bank CD	8.25	8.25
First National Bank BA	8.05	8.21
Highest-Yielding Commercial Paper	8.08	8.24
First National Bank Euro CD	8.30	8.30
First National Bank Euro TD	8.35	8.35

Appendix A

EXAMPLE ANSWERS

CHAPTER TWO

1. *Formula to Determine Cost of a T-Bill*

$$\frac{\text{Discount Amount}}{} = \frac{(\text{Face Value} \times \text{Discount Rate})}{360} \times \text{Number of Days to Maturity}$$

$$\text{Cost of a Bill} = \text{Face Value} - \text{Discount Amount}$$

Example

$$\text{Discount Amount} = \frac{(\$25,000 \times 8\%)}{360} \times 180$$

$$\text{Discount Amount} = \frac{(\$25,000 \times 8\%)}{360} \times 180$$

$$\text{Discount Amount} = \frac{\$2,000}{360} \times 180$$

Discount Amount = $1,000

Cost of Bill = $25,000 − $1,000

$$\text{Cost of Bill} = \$24{,}000$$

2. *Formula to Determine Interest Earned at Maturity for a Bill*

$$\text{Interest Earned} = \text{Discount Amount}$$

Example

$$\text{Interest Earned} = \$1{,}000$$

3. *Formula to Determine After-Tax Earnings*

$$\frac{\text{After-Tax}}{\text{Earnings}} = \text{Total Interest Earned} - \left(\text{Total Interest Earned} \times \text{Tax Rate}\right)$$

Example

$$\text{After-Tax Earnings} = \$1{,}000 - (\$1{,}000 \times 28\%)$$

$$\text{After-Tax Earnings} = \$1{,}000 - (\$1{,}000 \times .28)$$

$$\text{After-Tax Earnings} = \$1{,}000 - \$280$$

$$\text{After-Tax Earnings} = \$720$$

Remember, T-Bills are state-tax-free.

4. *Formula to Determine Yield to Maturity on a T-Bill*

$$\frac{\text{Yield to}}{\text{Maturity}} = \frac{(\text{Face Value} - \text{Discount Cost})}{\text{Discount Cost}} \times \frac{365}{\text{Days to Maturity}}$$

Example Answers

Example

$$\text{Yield to Maturity} = \frac{(\$25{,}000 - \$24{,}000)}{\$24{,}000} \times \frac{365}{180}$$

$$\text{Yield to Maturity} = \frac{\$1{,}000}{\$24{,}000} \times 2.028$$

Yield to Maturity = .0844998 = 8.45%

5. Formula to Convert Bond Equivalent Yield into a CD Equivalent

$$\text{CD Equivalent Yield} = \text{Bond Equivalent Yield} \times \frac{360}{365}$$

Example

$$\text{CD Equivalent Yield} = 8.45\% \times \frac{360}{365}$$

CD Equivalent Yield = .0833424 = 8.33%

6. Formula to Determine Proceeds from the Sale of a Bill

$$\text{Discount Amount} = \frac{(\text{Face Value} \times \text{Discount Rate})}{360} \times \text{Number of Days to Maturity}$$

Proceeds From the Sale = Face Value − Discount Amount

Example

$$\text{Discount Amount} = \frac{(\$25{,}000 \times 7.72\%)}{360} \times 135$$

Appendix A

$$\text{Discount Amount} = \frac{(\$1{,}930)}{360} \times 135$$

$$\text{Discount Amount} = \$723.75$$

$$\text{Proceeds From the Sale} = \$25{,}000 - \$723.75$$

$$\text{Proceeds From the Sale} = \$24{,}276.25$$

7. *Formula to Determine Amount Earned on the Investment*

$$\text{Amount Earned} = \text{Proceeds From the Sale} - \text{Cost of Purchase}$$

Example

$$\text{Amount Earned} = \$24{,}276.25 - \$24{,}000$$

$$\text{Amount Earned} = \$276.25$$

CHAPTER THREE

1. *Formula to Determine the Cost of a Discount Note*

$$\text{Discount Amount} = \frac{(\text{Face Value} \times \text{Discount Rate})}{360} \times \text{Number of Days to Maturity}$$

$$\text{Cost of Discount Note} = \text{Face Value} - \text{Discount Amount}$$

Example

$$\text{Discount Amount} = \frac{(\$75{,}000 \times 7.87)}{360} \times 63$$

Example Answers

$$\text{Discount Amount} = \frac{(\$75{,}000 \times .0787)}{360} \times 63$$

$$\text{Discount Amount} = \frac{(\$5{,}902.50)}{360} \times 63$$

Discount Amount = $1,032.94

Cost = $75,000 − $1,032.94

Cost = $73,967.06

2. *Formula to Determine Interest Earned if Held to Maturity*

$$\text{Interest Earned} = \text{Discount Amount}$$

Example

Interest Earned = $1,032.94

3. *Interest Earned After Taxes (Remember earnings on FHLMC discount notes are subject to taxation by the federal and state governments):*

$1,032.94 − ($1,032.94 × 25%) − ($1,032.94 × 12%)

$1,032.94 − $258.24 − $123.95 = $650.75

4. *Formula to Determine Yield to Maturity on a Discount Note*

$$\text{Yield to Maturity} = \frac{(\text{Face Value} - \text{Discount Cost})}{\text{Discount Cost}} \times \frac{365}{\text{Days to Maturity}}$$

Example

$$\text{Yield to Maturity} = \frac{(\$75{,}000 - \$73{,}967.06)}{\$73{,}967.06} \times \frac{365}{63}$$

$$\text{Yield to Maturity} = \frac{(\$1{,}032.94)}{\$73{,}967.06} \times \frac{365}{63}$$

$$\text{Yield to Maturity} = .0139648 \times \frac{365}{63}$$

Yield to Maturity = .0809071 = 8.09%

5. *Formula to Convert Yield into a CD Equivalent Yield*

$$\text{CD Equivalent Yield} = \text{Bond Equivalent Yield} \times \frac{360}{365}$$

Example

$$\text{CD Equivalent Yield} = 8.09\% \times \frac{360}{365}$$

CD Equivalent Yield = .0797917 = 7.98%

6. *Formula to Determine Proceeds from a Sale of a Discount Note*

$$\text{Discount Amount} = \frac{(\text{Face Value} \times \text{Discount Rate})}{360} \times \text{Number of Days to Maturity}$$

Proceeds From the Sale = Face Value − Discount Amount

Example Answers

Example

$$\frac{\text{Discount}}{\text{Amount}} = \frac{(\$75{,}000 \times 7.61\%)}{360} \times 32$$

$$\frac{\text{Discount}}{\text{Amount}} = \frac{(\$75{,}000 \times .0761)}{360} \times 32$$

$$\frac{\text{Discount}}{\text{Amount}} = \frac{(\$5{,}707.50)}{360} \times 32$$

Discount Amount = $507.33

Proceeds From the Sale = $75,000 − $507.33

Proceeds From the Sale = $74,492.67

7. Formula to Determine the Amount Earned on the Investment

Amount Earned = Proceeds From Sale − Cost of Purchase

Example

Amount Earned = $74,492.67 − $73,967.06

Amount Earned = $525.61

CHAPTER FOUR

1. Formula to Determine Cost of a Newly Issued CD

Cost = Face Value

Example

$$\text{Cost} = \$175,\!000$$

2. *Formula to Determine Interest Earned if Held to Maturity*

$$\frac{\text{Interest}}{\text{Earned}} = \frac{(\text{Face Value} \times \text{Rate})}{360} \times \frac{\text{Number of Days}}{\text{to Maturity}}$$

Example

$$\frac{\text{Interest}}{\text{Earned}} = \frac{(\$175,\!000 \times 8.15\%)}{360} \times 75$$

$$\frac{\text{Interest}}{\text{Earned}} = \frac{(\$175,\!000 \times .0815)}{360} \times 75$$

$$\frac{\text{Interest}}{\text{Earned}} = \frac{\$14,\!262.50}{360} \times 75$$

$$\text{Interest Earned} = \$2,\!971.35$$

3. *Earnings After Taxes =*

$$\$2,\!971.35 - (\$2,\!971.35 \times 28\%) - (\$2,\!971.35 \times 10\%)$$

$$= \$2,\!971.35 - \$831.98 - \$297.14$$

$$= \$1,\!842.23$$

4. *Formula for Yield to Maturity*

$$\text{Yield to Maturity} = \text{Rate of Interest}$$

Example Answers

Example

$$\text{Yield to Maturity} = 8.15\%$$

5. *Formula to Convert Yield into a Bond Equivalent Yield*

$$\frac{\text{Bond Equivalent}}{\text{Yield}} = \frac{\text{CD Equivalent}}{\text{Yield}} \times \frac{365}{360}$$

Example

$$\frac{\text{Bond Equivalent}}{\text{Yield}} = 8.15\% \times \frac{365}{360}$$

$$\text{Bond Equivalent Yield} = .0826319 = 8.26\%$$

6. *Formula to Determine the Total Cost of a Secondary Deposit*

Step 1

$$\frac{\text{Price per \$1}}{\text{of Face Value}} = \frac{1 + \dfrac{\text{Original}}{\text{Coupon}} \times \left(\dfrac{\text{Original Issued}}{\text{Days to Maturity}} / 360\right)}{1 + \dfrac{\text{Yield}}{\text{Price}} \times \left(\dfrac{\text{Current Number of}}{\text{Days to Maturity}} / 360\right)}$$

Step 2

$$\frac{\text{Total Cost}}{\text{(or Proceeds)}} = \text{Face Value} \times \text{Price Per \$1 of Face Value}$$

Example

Step 1

$$\frac{\text{Price per \$1}}{\text{of Face Value}} = \frac{1 + 8.60\% \times (180/360)}{1 + 8.10\% \times (95/360)}$$

$$\frac{\text{Price per \$1}}{\text{of Face Value}} = \frac{1 + .086 \times (.5)}{1 + .081 \times (.2639)}$$

$$\frac{\text{Price per \$1}}{\text{of Face Value}} = \frac{1 + .043}{1 + .0213759}$$

Price Per $1 of Face Value = 1.0211715

Step 2

Total Cost = $1,000,000 × 1.0211715

Total Cost = $1,021,171.50

7. *Formula to Determine Accrued Interest on a Secondary Deposit*

$$\text{Accrued Interest} = \frac{(\text{Face Value} \times \text{Original Coupon})}{360} \times \text{Number of Days Since Issued}$$

Example

$$\text{Accrued Interest} = \frac{(\$1,000,000 \times 8.60)}{360} \times 85$$

$$\text{Accrued Interest} = \frac{(\$1,000,000 \times .086)}{360} \times 85$$

$$\text{Accrued Interest} = \frac{\$86,000}{360} \times 85$$

Example Answers

$$\text{Accrued Interest} = \$20{,}305.55$$

8. Formula to Determine Principal

$$\text{Principal} = \text{Total Cost} - \text{Accrued Interest}$$

Example

$$\text{Principal} = \$1{,}021{,}171.50 - \$20{,}305.55$$

$$\text{Principal} = \$1{,}000{,}865.95$$

9. Formula to Determine Interest Received if Held to Maturity

$$\frac{\text{Interest}}{\text{Received}} = \frac{(\text{Face Value} \times \text{Original Rate})}{360} \times \frac{\text{Total Number}}{\text{Days Outstanding}}$$

Example

$$\frac{\text{Interest}}{\text{Received}} = \frac{(\$1{,}000{,}000 \times 8.60\%)}{360} \times 180$$

$$\text{Interest Received} = \$43{,}000$$

CHAPTER FIVE

1. Formula to Determine the Cost of a BA

$$\frac{\text{Discount}}{\text{Amount}} = \frac{(\text{Face Value} \times \text{Discount Rate})}{360} \times \frac{\text{Number of Days}}{\text{to Maturity}}$$

$$\text{Cost} = \text{Face Amount} - \text{Discount Amount}$$

Example

$$\frac{\text{Discount}}{\text{Amount}} = \frac{(\$5,000,000 \times 7.99\%)}{360} \times 120$$

$$\frac{\text{Discount}}{\text{Amount}} = \frac{\$399,500}{360} \times 120$$

Discount Amount = $133,166.66

Cost = $5,000,000 − $133,166.66

Cost = $4,866,833.34

2. *Formula to Determine Interest Earned if Held to Maturity*

Interest Earned = Discount Amount

Example

Interest Earned = $133,166.66

3. *Earnings After Taxes =*

$133,166.66 − ($133,166.66 × 26%) − ($133,166.66 × 11%)

= $133,166.66 − $34,623.33 − $14,648.33

= $83,895

4. *Formula to Determine CD Equivalent Yield to Maturity*

Example Answers

$$\text{Yield to Maturity} = \frac{\text{Discount}}{(\text{Face Amount} - \text{Discount})} \times \frac{360}{\text{Days to Maturity}}$$

Example

$$\text{Yield to Maturity} = \frac{\$133{,}166.66}{(\$5{,}000{,}000 - \$133{,}166.66)} \times \frac{360}{120}$$

$$\text{Yield to Maturity} = \frac{\$133{,}166.66}{\$4{,}866{,}833.34} \times \frac{360}{120}$$

Yield to Maturity = .0274 × 360/120 = .0822 = 8.22%

5. *Formula to Convert CD Equivalent into a Bond Equivalent Yield*

$$\text{Bond Equivalent Yield} = \text{CD Equivalent Yield} \times \frac{365}{360}$$

Example

$$\text{Bond Equivalent Yield} = 8.22\% \times \frac{365}{360}$$

Bond Equivalent Yield = .0833 = 8.33%

6. *Formula to Determine the Proceeds of a Sale of a BA*

$$\text{Discount Amount} = \frac{(\text{Face Value} \times \text{Discount Rate})}{360} \times \text{Number of Days to Maturity}$$

Proceeds = Face Value − Discount Amount

Example

$$\frac{\text{Discount}}{\text{Amount}} = \frac{(\$5{,}000{,}000 \times 8.12\%)}{360} \times 73$$

$$\frac{\text{Discount}}{\text{Amount}} = \frac{\$406{,}000}{360} \times 73$$

Discount Amount = $82,327.77

Proceeds = $5,000,000 − $82,327.77

Proceeds = $4,917,672.23

7. *Formula to Determine Earnings from the Investment*

$$\text{Earnings} = \text{Proceeds of the Sale} - \text{Cost of Purchase}$$

Example

Earnings = $4,917,672.23 − $4,866,833.34

Earnings = $50,838.89

CHAPTER SIX

1. *Formula to Determine Cost of Discounted Commercial Paper*

$$\frac{\text{Discount}}{\text{Amount}} = \frac{(\text{Face Value} \times \text{Discount Rate})}{360} \times \frac{\text{Number of Days}}{\text{to Maturity}}$$

Cost = Face Value − Discount Amount

Example Answers

Example

$$\text{Discount Amount} = \frac{(\$250{,}000 \times 8.55\%)}{360} \times 30$$

$$\text{Discount Amount} = \frac{\$21{,}375}{360} \times 30$$

Discount Amount = $1,781.25

Cost = $250,000 − $1,781.25

Cost = $248,218.75

2. Formula to Determine Interest Earned

$$\text{Interest Earned} = \text{Discount Amount}$$

Example

$$\text{Interest Earned} = \$1{,}781.25$$

3. Interest Earned After Taxes =

$$\$1{,}781.25 - (\$1{,}781.25 \times 26\%) - (\$1{,}781.25 \times 11\%)$$

$$= \$1{,}781.25 - \$463.13 - \$195.94$$

$$= \$1{,}122.18$$

4. Formula to Determine Yield to Maturity on Discounted CP

$$\text{Yield to Maturity} = \frac{\text{Discount}}{(\text{Face Amount} - \text{Discount})} \times \frac{360}{\text{Days to Maturity}}$$

Example

$$\text{Yield to Maturity} = \frac{\$1{,}781.25}{(\$250{,}000 - \$1{,}781.25)} \times \frac{360}{30}$$

$$\text{Yield to Maturity} = \frac{\$1{,}781.25}{(\$248{,}218.75)} \times \frac{360}{30}$$

$$\text{Yield to Maturity} = .0861132 = 8.61\%$$

5. Formula to Convert From CD to Bond Equivalent Yield

$$\text{Bond Equivalent Yield} = \text{CD Equivalent Yield} \times \frac{365}{360}$$

Example

$$\text{Bond Equivalent Yield} = 8.61\% \times \frac{365}{360}$$

$$\text{Bond Equivalent Yield} = .0872958 = 8.73\%$$

6. Formula to Determine Cost of Interest Bearing Commercial Paper

$$\text{Cost} = \text{Face Value}$$

Example

$$\text{Cost} = \$250{,}000$$

Example Answers

7. Formula to Determine Interest on Interest Bearing CP

$$\frac{\text{Interest}}{\text{Earned}} = \frac{(\text{Rate} \times \text{Face} \times \text{Number of Days to Maturity}/360)}{\text{Face} - (\text{Rate} \times \text{Face} \times \text{Number of Days to Maturity}/360)} \times \text{Face}$$

Example

$$\frac{\text{Interest}}{\text{Earned}} = \frac{(8.55\% \times \$250{,}000 \times 30/360)}{\$250{,}000 - (8.55\% \times \$250{,}000 \times 30/360)} \times \$250{,}000$$

$$\frac{\text{Interest}}{\text{Earned}} = \frac{(.0855 \times \$250{,}000 \times 30/360)}{\$250{,}000 - (.0855 \times \$250{,}000 \times 30/360)} \times \$250{,}000$$

$$\frac{\text{Interest}}{\text{Earned}} = \frac{\$1{,}781.25}{\$250{,}000 - \$1{,}781.25} \times \$250{,}000$$

$$\frac{\text{Interest}}{\text{Earned}} = \frac{\$1{,}781.25}{\$248{,}218.75} \times \$250{,}000$$

Interest Earned = .0071761 × $250,000

Interest Earned = $1,794.03

8. After Tax Earnings =

$1,794.03 − ($1,794.03 × 26%) − ($1,794.03 × 11%)

= $1,794.03 − $466.45 − $197.34

= $1,130.24

9. Formula to Determine Yield on Interest Bearing CP

$$\frac{\text{Yield to}}{\text{Maturity}} = \frac{\text{Interest Earned}}{\text{Face Value}} \times \frac{360}{\text{Number of Days to Maturity}}$$

Example

$$\frac{\text{Yield to}}{\text{Maturity}} = \frac{\$1{,}794.03}{\$250{,}000} \times \frac{360}{30}$$

Yield to Maturity = .0861132 = 8.61%

10. *Formula to Convert From CD to Bond Equivalent Yield*

$$\frac{\text{Bond Equivalent}}{\text{Yield}} = \frac{\text{CD Equivalent}}{\text{Yield}} \times \frac{365}{360}$$

Example

$$\frac{\text{Bond Equivalent}}{\text{Yield}} = 8.61\% \times \frac{365}{360}$$

Bond Equivalent Yield = .0872958 = 8.73%

CHAPTER SEVEN

1. *Formula to Determine Cost of an RP*

Cost = Face Value

Example

Cost = $100,000

Example Answers

2. Formula to Determine Interest Earned on an RP

$$\frac{\text{Interest}}{\text{Earned}} = \frac{(\text{Face Value} \times \text{Rate})}{360} \times \frac{\text{Number of Days}}{\text{to Maturity}}$$

Example

$$\frac{\text{Interest}}{\text{Earned}} = \frac{(\$100{,}000 \times 8.10\%)}{360} \times 3$$

$$\frac{\text{Interest}}{\text{Earned}} = \frac{(\$8{,}100)}{360} \times 3$$

$$\text{Interest Earned} = \$67.50$$

3. Earnings After Tax =

$$\$67.50 - (\$67.50 \times 26\%) - (\$67.50 \times 11\%)$$

$$= \$67.50 - \$17.55 - \$7.43$$

$$= \$42.52$$

4. Formula to Determine Yield to Maturity

$$\text{Yield to Maturity} = \text{Rate}$$

Example

$$\text{Yield to Maturity} = 8.10\%$$

CHAPTER EIGHT — CASE STUDY

First, we know from looking at the lists in Appendix B that all the securities listed meet KJB's restrictions. Each security is available for $1,000,000, each offers three month maturities, and each is guaranteed by either the U.S. government, a U.S. government agency, the largest local bank (First National Bank), or a large U.S.-based company. A repurchase agreement also would fit KJB's parameters, if Bradley could find an institution willing to offer one with a three-month maturity. Since these are not always available, we will ignore repos for this example. KJB's state does not tax the earnings of securities owned by companies, so Bradley can ignore state taxes as a means of comparison. This leaves liquidity and yield to maturity for Bradley to compare in making his decision.

Let's look at yield first. Bradley is given the price and CD equivalent yield quotes on the securities that fit his parameters. Remember, all yields must be on a similar basis for the comparison to be accurate. Normally some of the yields are quoted on a CD equivalent basis while others are quoted on a bond equivalent basis, but in this case all yields are presented as CD equivalents. You can assume that the salesman has done all the necessary conversions for you.

Now Bradley can accurately compare the securities' yields. He sees that Euro TDs, with a CD yield of 8.35 percent, offer the highest return. Euro TDs, however, do not have a secondary market and therefore are not a liquid investment. Bradley believes that he will not need the $1,000,000 during the three-month investment period but he has stated his desire to own a relatively liquid investment in case the unforeseen need to liquidate arises. Therefore, Bradley would probably choose not to invest in Euro TDs although they offer the highest yield.

The next highest yielding security is First National Bank's Euro CD at 8.30 percent. Unlike Euro TDs, Euro CDs offer Bradley liquidity because of their active secondary market. Although not nearly as liquid as a T-Bill or a discount note, First National Bank's Euro CD could be sold easily if necessary. Bradley probably would purchase this Euro CD since it offers the highest yield of the securities that meet his requirements.

Example Answers

The most important thing to remember is that every investor has different biases, limitations, and restrictions. In this case, Bradley was looking for the highest yielding security that offered liquidity, was backed by the guarantors chosen by his superiors, and matured in three months. The First National Bank Euro CD fit these parameters and offered the highest yield of the acceptable securities.

Another investor might not agree with the choice. One investor, looking at the yield choices, might have picked the Euro TD because it offers the highest yield. For this investor liquidity might not be important. Still another investor might require more additional yield on a Euro CD compared to a T-Bill or discount note. In this example, the difference in yield between the Euro CD and the Bill is .44 percent (8.30 percent − 7.86 percent). Perhaps this other investor would only invest in the less safe, less liquid Euro CD if it offered more additional yield than .44 percent.

Appendix B

SUMMARY

U.S. TREASURY BILLS

Guarantor	U.S. Government
Denominations	Minimum: $10,000 Increments: $5,000
Original Maturities	3 Months, 6 Months, 1 Year Cash Managements: Various
Tax Effect	Taxable : Federal State- and Local-Tax-Free
Interest Payments	Purchased at a Discount, Face Value Received at Maturity
Form of Ownership	Book-entry

FEDERAL FARM CREDIT BANK DISCOUNT NOTES

Guarantor	Farm Credit Banks
Denominations	Minimum: $5,000 Increments: $5,000
Original Maturities	5 Days To 1 Year
Tax Effect	Taxable: Federal State- and Local-Tax-Free
Interest Payments	Purchased at a Discount, Face Value Received at Maturity
Form of Ownership	Book-entry

FEDERAL NATIONAL MORTGAGE ASSOCIATION DISCOUNT NOTES

Guarantor	Federal National Mortgage Ass.
Denominations	Minimum: $10,000 Increments: $5,000
Original Maturities	30 Days To 1 Year
Tax Effect	Taxable: Federal, State, and Local
Interest Payments	Purchased at a Discount, Face Value Received at Maturity
Form of Ownership	Book-entry

Summary

FEDERAL HOME LOAN BANK DISCOUNT NOTES

Guarantor	Federal Home Loan Banks
Denominations	Minimum: $100,000 Increments: $5,000
Original Maturities	30 Days To 1 Year
Tax Effect	Taxable: Federal State- and Local-Tax-Free
Interest Payments	Purchased at a Discount, Face Value Received at Maturity
Form of Ownership	Book-entry

FEDERAL HOME LOAN MORTGAGE CORPORATION DISCOUNT NOTES

Guarantor	Federal Home Loan Mortgage Corporation
Denominations	Minimum: $25,000 Increments: $1,000
Original Maturities	Through 1 Year
Tax Effects	Taxable: Federal, State, and Local
Interest Payments	Purchased at a Discount, Face Value Received at Maturity
Form of Ownership	Book-entry

NEGOTIABLE CERTIFICATES OF DEPOSIT

Guarantor	Issuing Institution FDIC-Insured up to $100,000
Denominations (Most Common)	Minimum: $100,000 Increments: Any Most Common Minimum Traded In Secondary Market: $1,000,000
Original Maturities	7 Days To 5 Years
Tax Effects	Taxable: Federal, State, and Local
Interest Payments	Most Common: At Maturity Semi-annual When Maturing 1 Year or Longer May Be Purchased at a Discount
Form of Ownership	Bearer or Registered Book-entry Available For Non- negotiable

EURO CERTIFICATES OF DEPOSIT

Guarantor	Parent of the Issuing Institution
Denominations	Minimum :$1,000,000 Most Commonly Traded in Amounts of $5,000,000
Original Maturities	1 Month To 5 Years
Tax Effects	Taxable: Federal, State, and Local

Summary

Interest Payments	At Maturity Semi-annual if Maturing 1 Year or Longer
Form Of Ownership	Bearer

EURO TIME DEPOSITS

Guarantor	Parent of the Issuing Institution
Denominations (Most Common)	Minimum: $100,000 Increments: Any
Original Maturities	1 Day Through Several Years Typically 1 Day Through 6 Months
Tax Effects	Taxable: Federal, State, and Local
Interest Payments	At Maturity
Form of Ownership	Book-entry

BANKERS ACCEPTANCES

Guarantor	Accepting Bank Bank's Initiating Customer Goods In Transit, If Applicable
Denominations (Most Common)	Minimum: $100,000 Possible to Find Smaller

	Increments: Any
	Minimum Traded: $500,000 or $1,000,000
Original Maturities (Most Common)	1 Month To 6 Months
Tax Effects	Taxable: Federal, State, and Local
Interest Payments	Purchased at a Discount, Face Value Received at Maturity
Form of Ownership	Bearer

COMMERCIAL PAPER

Guarantor	Issuing Company Frequently Backed by Bank's Letter of Credit
Denominations (Most Common)	Minimum: $25,000 or $100,000, Depending On Issuer Increments: Any
Original Maturities	1 Day to 270 Days
Tax Effects	Taxable: Federal, State, and Local
Interest Payments	At Maturity or Discounted
Form of Ownership	Book-entry or Bearer

REPURCHASE AGREEMENTS

Guarantor	Originating Institution and Backed by Securities as Collateral
Denominations (Most Common)	Minimum: $100,000 Increments: Any
Original Maturities	Theoretically Any Most Common: 1 Day to 30 Days Open Maturity Contracts Available
Tax Effects	Taxable: Federal, State, and Local
Interest Payments	At Maturity
Form of Ownership (Most Common)	Book-entry

Appendix C

CHARACTERISTICS CROSS REFERENCE

GUARANTOR

U.S. Government

    U.S. Treasury Bills

Agency of the U.S. Government

    Federal Farm Credit Bank Discount Notes
    Federal National Mortgage Association Discount Notes
    Federal Home Loan Bank Discount Notes
    Federal Home Loan Mortgage Corporation Discount Notes

Financial Institutions

    Certificates of Deposits
    Euro Certificates of Deposits
    Euro Time Deposits
    Bankers Acceptances

Repurchase Agreements

Company

Commercial Paper

MINIMUM DENOMINATION (MOST COMMON)

$5,000

Federal Farm Credit Bank Discount Notes

$10,000

U.S. Treasury Bills
Federal National Mortgage Association Discount Notes

$25,000

Federal Home Loan Mortgage Corporation Discount Notes
Some Commercial Paper

$100,000

Negotiable Certificates of Deposit
Commercial Paper
Federal Home Loan Bank Discount Notes
Euro Time Deposits
Bankers Acceptances
Repurchase Agreements

Characteristics Cross Reference

$1,000,000

    Euro Certificate of Deposits

EARLIEST ORIGINAL MATURITY

1 Day

    Commercial Paper
    Euro Time Deposits
    Repurchase Agreements
    Federal Home Loan Mortgage Corporation Discount Notes

5 Days

    Federal Farm Credit Bank Discount Notes

7 Days

    Certificates of Deposit

1 Month

    Bankers Acceptances
    Euro Certificates of Deposit
    Federal Home Loan Bank Discount Notes
    Federal National Mortgage Association Discount Notes

3 Months

    U.S. Treasury Bills

LONGEST ORIGINAL MATURITY

1 Month

    Repurchase Agreements (Most Common)

6 Months

    Bankers Acceptances

270 Days

    Commercial Paper

1 Year

    U.S. Treasury Bills
    Federal Farm Credit Bank Discount Notes
    Federal National Mortgage Association Discount Notes
    Federal Home Loan Bank Discount Notes
    Federal Home Loan Mortgage Corporation Discount Notes

5 Years

    Certificates of Deposit
    Euro Certificates of Deposit
    Euro Time Deposits

Characteristics Cross Reference

TAX EFFECTS

Taxable: Federal, State, and Local

Federal National Mortgage Association Discount Notes
Federal Home Loan Mortgage Corporation Discount Notes
Certificates of Deposit
Euro Certificates of Deposit
Euro Time Deposits
Bankers Acceptances
Commercial Paper
Repurchase Agreements

Taxable: Federal Only

U.S. Treasury Bills
Federal Farm Credit Bank Discount Notes
Federal Home Loan Bank Discount Notes

FORMS OF OWNERSHIP

Book-Entry

U.S. Treasury Bills
Federal Farm Credit Bank Discount Notes
Federal National Mortgage Association Discount Notes
Federal Home Loan Bank Discount Notes
Federal Home Loan Mortgage Corporation Discount Notes
Certificates of Deposit
Euro Time Deposits
Commercial Paper
Repurchase Agreements

Bearer

    Negotiable Certificates of Deposit
    Euro Certificates of Deposit
    Bankers Acceptances
    Commercial Paper

Registered

    Certificates of Deposit

FORM OF INTEREST PAYMENTS

Interest at Maturity

    Certificates of Deposit
    Euro Certificates of Deposit
    Euro Time Deposits
    Commercial Paper
    Repurchase Agreements

Discount

    U.S. Treasury Bills
    Federal Farm Credit Bank Discount Notes
    Federal National Mortgage Association Discount Notes
    Federal Home Loan Bank Discount Notes
    Federal Home Loan Mortgage Corporation Discount Notes
    Certificates of Deposit
    Bankers Acceptances
    Commercial Paper

Appendix D

CHARACTERISTICS CROSS REFERENCE MATRICES

MINIMUM DENOMINATIONS	GUARANTOR		
	U.S. Government	Agency of U.S. Gov't	Financial Institution	Company
$1,000,000			Euro CD	
$100,000		FHLB Discount Note	Negotiable CD Euro Time Deposit Bankers Acceptance Repurchase Agreement	Commercial Paper
$25,000		FHLMC Discount Note		Commercial Paper
$10,000	U.S. T-Bills	FNMA Discount Note		
$5,000		FFCB Discount Note		

ORIGINAL MATURITIES / GUARANTOR

	U.S. Government	Agency of U.S. Gov't	Financial Institution	Company
5 Years			CD Euro CD Euro TD	
1 Year	U.S. T-Bill	All Discount Notes	CD Euro CD Euro TD	
9 Months		All Discount Notes	CD Euro CD Euro TD	Commercial Paper
6 Months	U.S. T-Bill	All Discount Notes	CD, BA Euro CD Euro TD	Commercial Paper
3 Months	U.S. T-Bill	All Discount Notes	CD, BA Euro CD Euro TD	Commercial Paper
1 Month		All Discount Notes	CD, BA Euro CD, Repos Euro TD	Commercial Paper
1 Week		FFCB Discount Note FHLMC Discount Note	CD Euro TD Repos	Commercial Paper
5 Days		FFCB Discount Note FHLMC Discount Note	Euro TD Repos	Commercial Paper
1 Day		FHLMC Discount Note	Euro TD Repos	Commercial Paper

	U.S. Government	Agency of U.S. Gov't	Financial Institution	Company
Taxable: Federal	U.S. T-Bill	FFCB Discount Note FHLB Discount Note		
Taxable: Federal, State and Local		FNMA Discount Note FHLMC Discount Note	CD Euro CD Euro TD BA Repo	Commercial Paper

GUARANTOR

TAX EFFECT

AVAILABLE FORM OF OWNERSHIP

	U.S. Government	Agency of U.S. Gov't	Financial Institution	Company
Book-Entry	U.S. T-Bill	All Discount Notes	CD Euro TD Repo	Commercial Paper
Bearer			Negotiable CD Euro CD BA	Commercial Paper
Registered			CD	

GUARANTOR

	U.S. Government	Agency of U.S. Gov't	Financial Institution	Company
Interest at Maturity			CD Euro CD Euro TD Repo	Commercial Paper
Discount	U.S. T-Bill	All Discount Notes	CD BA	Commercial Paper

GUARANTOR

INTEREST PAYMENTS

ORIGINAL MATURITIES	$5,000	$10,000	$25,000	$100,000	$1,000,000
5 Years				CD Euro TD	Euro CD
1 Year	FFCB Discount Note	T-Bill FNMA Discount Note	FHLMC Discount Note	FHLB Discount Note CD, Euro TD	Euro CD
9 Months	FFCB Discount Note	FNMA Discount Note	Commercial Paper FHLMC Discount Note	FHLB Discount Note CD, Euro TD Commercial Paper	Euro CD
6 Months	FFCB Discount Note	T-Bill FNMA Discount Note	Commercial Paper FHLMC Discount Note	FHLB Discount Note CD, Euro TD BA, Commercial Paper	Euro CD
3 Months	FFCB Discount Note	T-Bill FNMA Discount Note	Commercial Paper FHLMC Discount Note	FHLB Discount Note CD, Euro TD BA, Commercial Paper	Euro CD
1 Month	FFCB Discount Note	FNMA Discount Note	Commercial Paper FHLMC Discount Note	FHLB Discount Note CD, Euro TD, Repo Commercial Paper, BA	Euro CD
1 Week	FFCB Discount Note		Commercial Paper FHLMC Discount Note	CD, Repo Euro TD Commercial Paper	
5 Days	FFCB Discount Note		Commercial Paper FHLMC Discount Note	Euro TD Commercial Paper Repo	
1 Day			Commercial Paper FHLMC Discount Note	Euro TD Commercial Paper Repo	

MINIMUM DENOMINATIONS

MINIMUM DENOMINATIONS

TAX EFFECT					
Taxable: Federal	FFCB Discount Note	T-Bill		FHLB Discount Note	
Taxable: Federal, State, and Local		FNMA Discount Note	Commercial Paper FHLMC Discount Note	CD, Euro TD, BA, Commercial Paper Repo	Euro CD
	$5,000	$10,000	$25,000	$100,000	$1,000,000

AVAILABLE FORM OF OWNERSHIP

Book-Entry	FFCB Discount Note	T-Bill FNMA Discount Note	Commercial Paper FHLMC Discount Note	FHLB Discount Note CD, Euro TD Commercial Paper Repo	
Bearer			Commercial Paper	Negotiable CD, BA, Commercial Paper	Euro CD
Registered				CD	
	$5,000	$10,000	$25,000	$100,000	$1,000,000

MINIMUM DENOMINATIONS

MINIMUM DENOMINATIONS

Interest at Maturity			Commercial Paper	CD, Euro TD Commercial Paper Repo	Euro CD
Discount	FFCB Discount Note	T-Bill FNMA Discount Note	Commercial Paper FHLMC Discount Notes	FHLB Discount Note CD, BA, Commercial Paper	
	$5,000	$10,000	$25,000	$100,000	$1,000,000

INTEREST PAYMENTS

ORIGINAL MATURITIES		
5 Years		Euro TD, CD Euro CD
1 Year	FFCE Discount Note T-Bill FHLB Discount Note	Euro TD, FHLMC Discount Note FNMA Discount Note, CD, Euro CD
9 Months	FFCB Discount Note FHLB Discount Note	Commercial Paper, Euro CD, Euro TD, FHLMC Discount Note, FNMA Discount Note, CD
6 Months	FFCB Discount Note T-Bill FHLE Discount Note	Commercial Paper, Euro CD, Euro TD, BA FHLMC Discount Note, FNMA Discount Note, CD
3 Months	FFCB Discount Note T-Bill FHLB Discount Note	Commercial Paper, Euro CD, Euro TD, BA FHLMC Discount Note, FNMA Discount Note, CD
1 Month	FFCB Discount Note FHLB Discount Note	Commercial Paper, Euro CD, Euro TD, BA, Repo FHLMC Discount Note, FNMA Discount Note, CD
1 Week	FFCB Discount Note	Commercial Paper, Euro TD, Repo FHLMC Discount Note, CD
5 Days	FFCB Discount Note	Commercial Paper, Euro TD, Repo FHLMC Discount Note, CD
1 Day		Commercial Paper, Euro TD, Repo FHLMC Discount Note
	Taxable: **Federal**	**Taxable:** **Federal, State, and Local**

TAX EFFECTS

AVAILABLE FORM OF OWNERSHIP

ORIGINAL MATURITIES	Book-Entry	Bearer	Registered
5 Years	CD, Euro TD	Euro CD	CD
1 Year	T-Bill; FFCB, FHLMC, FHLB, FNMA Discount Notes; CD; Euro TD	Negotiable CD, Euro CD	CD
9 Months	FFCB, FHLMC, FHLB, FNMA Discount Notes; CD; Euro TD; Commercial Paper	Negotiable CD, Euro CD, Commercial Paper	CD
6 Months	T-Bill; FFCB, FHLMC, FHLB, FNMA Discount Notes; CD; Euro TD, Commercial Paper	Negotiable CD, Euro CD, BA Commercial Paper	CD
3 Months	T-Bill; All Discount Notes; CD; Euro TD, Commercial Paper	Negotiable CD, Euro CD, BA Commercial Paper	CD
1 Month	FFCB, FHLMC, FHLB, FNMA Discount Notes; Repos; CD; Euro TD, Commercial Paper	Negotiable CD, Euro CD, BA Commercial Paper	CD
1 Week	FFCB, FHLMC Discount Notes; Repos; CD; Euro TD; Commercial Paper	Negotiable CD, Commercial Paper	CD
5 Days	FFCB, FHLMC Discount Notes; Repos; Euro TD; Commercial Paper	Commercial Paper	
1 Day	FHLMC Discount Note; Repos; Euro TD; Commercial Paper	Commercial Paper	

	Interest at Maturity	INTEREST PAYMENTS	Discount
5 Years	CD, Euro CD, Euro TD		
1 Year	CD, Euro CD, Euro TD		T-Bill; FFCB, FHLMC, FHLB, FNMA Discount Notes; CD
9 Months	CD, Euro CD, Euro TD, Commercial Paper		FFCB, FHLMC, FHLB, FNMA Discount Notes; CD; Commercial Paper
6 Months	CD, Euro CD, Euro TD, Commercial Paper		T-Bill; FFCB, FHLMC, FHLB, FNMA Discount Notes; CD; BA; Commercial Paper
3 Months	CD, Euro CD, Euro TD, Commercial Paper		T-Bill; FFCB, FHLMC, FHLB, FNMA Discount Notes; CD; BA; Commercial Paper
1 Month	CD, Euro CD, Euro TD, Commercial Paper, Repos		FFCB, FHLMC, FHLB, FNMA Discount Notes; CD; BA; Commercial Paper
1 Week	CD, Euro TD, Commercial Paper, Repos		FFCB, FHLMC Discount Notes; CD; Commercial Paper
5 Days	Euro TD, Commercial Paper, Repos		FFCB, FHLMC Discount Notes; Commercial Paper
1 Day	Euro TD, Commercial Paper, Repos		FHLMC Discount Note, Commercial Paper

ORIGINAL MATURITIES

AVAILABLE FORM OF OWNERSHIP

TAX EFFECT	Book-Entry	Bearer	Registered
Taxable: Federal	T-Bill, FFCB Discount Note, FHLB Discount Note		
Taxable: Federal, State, and Local	FNMA Discount Note, FHLMC Discount Note, CD, Euro TD, Commercial Paper, Repurchase Agreements	CD, Euro CD, BA, Commercial Paper	CD

AVAILABLE FORM OF OWNERSHIP

	Book-Entry	Bearer	Registered
Interest at Maturity	CD, Euro TD, Commercial Paper, Repurchase Agreement	CD, Euro CD, Commercial Paper	CD
Discount	T-Bill, All Discount Notes, CD, Commercial Paper	CD, BA, Commercial Paper	CD

INTEREST PAYMENTS

INTEREST PAYMENTS

		TAX EFFECT
Interest at Maturity	T-Bill, FFCB Discount Note, FHLB Discount Note	CD, Euro CD, Euro TD, Commercial Paper, Repurchase Agreement
Discount		CD, FNMA Discount Note, FHLMC Discount Note, BA, Commercial Paper
	Taxable: Federal	**Taxable: Federal, State, and Local**

Appendix E

TAX EFFECTS

It cannot be over-emphasized that investors, whether they are individuals or companies, should consult their tax accountant in determining which tax rules and rates affect the income received from securities. The returns received, and the way alternative securities compare, can be greatly altered by the impact of these rules and rates on the investor. There is only one federal government with its rules, regulations, and rates, but there are fifty different states, and various U.S. territories, each with its own set of rules and rates.

A prime example of the point being made here is the case of state taxation on the income corporations receive on "state-tax-free" securities. Some states define their tax on corporations in ways other than an income tax. They may tax a corporation's income on securities as if the securities were state-taxable even though for individuals such income would not be taxed. On the other hand, some states do not tax the earnings on securities that theoretically are subject to state taxation. Therefore, knowing which rules affect you can significantly influence your choice of security.

Appendix F

GLOSSARY

Accrued Interest on a security with a stated coupon rate, the amount of interest earned by holders of that security at a certain point in time, either since the security was first issued or since the last coupon payment.

Asked (offer) Price price at which sellers of a security are willing to sell.

Arbitrage simultaneous purchase and sale of the same, similar or different securities in such a way as to take advantage of price movement differentials in separate markets, maturities, etc.

Bankers Acceptances (BA) discounted, negotiable security representing a foreign or domestic bank's commitment to back a draft drawn on the bank's customer to provide a specific sum of money, at a specific date to a third party. Used to facilitate foreign trade.

Basis Point equal to 1/100 of 1%. Typically used to describe the movement of interest rates. If a security's yield is 8% today and 8.10% tomorrow, it is said to have moved 10 basis points.

Bearer form of ownership of a security whose certificate states the terms of the debt, but does not identify the owner's name and is thus considered negotiable.

Bear Market expression used to describe the general downward trend in prices in any particular market.

Bid-Asked Spread the difference between the price at which one is willing to sell (asked, or offered price) and the price at which one is willing to buy (bid).

Bid Price price of a particular security where buyers are willing to buy.

Bond Equivalent Yield yield used to accurately compare securities with the yields on coupon bonds, based on a 365-day year.

Book-Entry form of ownership whose proof is in a paperless computer entry and investor confirmation.

Bull Market expression used to describe the general upward trend in prices in any particular market.

Cash Flow the difference between the income of funds into an entity and its outflows for expenses and debt service.

Cash Settlement Monies and securities are exchanged the same day that the transaction is completed.

Certificates of Deposit (CD) obligation of a financial institution that promises to repay principal plus interest on funds which are left on deposit at the institution for a specific length of time.

Commercial Paper Short-term unsecured obligation issued by corporations, finance companies or bank holding companies.

Glossary

Compound Interest interest paid on the principal and previous earned interest.

Corporate Settlement Monies and securities are exchanged five business days after the transaction is completed.

Coupon Payment periodic (typically every six months) payment of interest based on the stated coupon rate of interest assigned to the security and its par value.

Coupon Rate interest payment rate assigned to a security when it is first issued.

CUSIP short for Committee on Uniform Security Identification Procedure. Refers to a number assigned to a security for identification purposes. Can be found by an investor on the confirmation statement.

Debenture bond which is secured by the general credit of the issuing entity.

Default Risk the possibility that the guarantor of the debt obligation will fail to meet the payment commitments.

Deflation a decrease in the general level of prices.

Denomination face amount stated on a certificate or par amount on a confirmation statement that the issuer will pay at maturity.

Discount CDs time deposit obligation, issued by a financial institution on a discount basis, where the full face value is paid at maturity.

Discounted Security a security whose principal price is either below par or below its face value.

Diversification dividing investable funds between different types of securities and issuers to reduce the risk to the total portfolio.

Euro Dollar Certificate of Deposit U.S. dollar denominated certificate of deposit issued outside of the U.S. either by a foreign branch of a U.S. bank or by a non-U.S. bank.

Euro Time Deposits (Euro TDs) U.S. dollars deposited with a stated maturity and rate outside the U.S., either in a foreign bank or in a foreign branch of a domestic bank.

Face Value (Par Value) for a discounted security that amount which the investor will receive at maturity. For an interest bearing security, that amount that the investor will receive as principal at maturity, or the principal value of the bond if its coupon rate and yield to maturity were equal.

"Fannie Mae" name commonly used to refer to the Federal National Mortgage Association and its debt issues.

Federal Deposit Insurance Corporation (FDIC) the federal bank agency which insures the deposits of member banks up to $100,000.

Federal Farm Credit Banks (FFCB) private cooperatively owned, federally chartered and sponsored nationwide system of banks and associations that provides mortgage loans, short and intermediate-term credit and related services to farmers, ranchers and other related businesses.

Federal Farm Credit Bank Debentures obligation of the Federal Farm Credit Banks initially issued to mature between three months and fifteen years.

Federal Farm Credit Bank Discount Notes a short-term discounted obligation of the Federal Farm Credit Banks with an initial maturity of one year or less.

Glossary

Federal Home Loan Bank bank set up to operate as a central credit reserve system for the thrift industry.

Federal Home Loan Bank Debentures obligations of the Federal Home Loan Bank with initial maturities, typically between one and ten years.

Federal Home Loan Bank Discount Notes short-term, discounted obligations of the Federal Home Loan Bank with initial maturities of one year or less.

Federal Home Loan Mortgage Corporation (FHLMC) U.S. Government sponsored agency whose purpose is to aid the funding of home mortgages, by acting as a conduit between originators of mortgages and the securities market.

Federal Home Loan Mortgage Corporation Discount Note short-term, unsecured, discounted obligation of FHLMC issued to mature in one year or less.

Federal National Mortgage Association (FNMA) U.S. Government sponsored agency set up to provide liquidity to the home mortgage market.

Federal National Mortgage Association Debenture obligation of FNMA initially issued to mature between one and ten years.

Federal National Mortgage Association Discount Note short-term, discounted obligation of FNMA initially issued to mature in one year or less.

"Freddie Mac" name commonly used to refer to the Federal Home Loan Mortgage Corporation and its debt issues.

Full Faith and Credit term commonly used to describe the safety and taxing powers of a government entity, typically the U.S. Government.

Inflation an increase in the general level of prices.

Interest Rate Risk chance that a security's value will alter due to a general change in interest rates.

Interest Payments funds received from a debt issuer as a return for the lending of funds for a specific period of time.

Issue Date date which a security first starts earning interest.

Liquidity ability of converting a debt obligation into cash.

Liquidity Risk the chance that a non-cash asset cannot be easily converted into cash.

Long Position expression commonly used to refer to owning one or more securities.

Market Value the price that a security can receive in its particular market at the present time.

Matrix a grid formed from the columns of the horizontal axis and the rows of the vertical axis of a graph to give a two-dimensional view of the relationship between two characteristics.

Maturity Date date when the issuer of the security agrees to pay back the principal of the debt obligation along with either interest or the last coupon payment.

Money Market the market of debt obligations of maturities of one year or less.

Money Market (CD) Equivalent Yield typically stated on a 360 day year basis, the yield most associated with one year and under maturity obligations of banks and corporations.

Glossary

Mutual Fund a type of investment company that pools funds to purchase specific types of securities and gives investors a fractional ownership share in the newly created portfolio.

Premium a security whose market price is over its face value.

Primary Certificate of Deposit a newly issued certificate of deposit.

Registered Bond bond with the owner's name identified on the certificate and reported to tax authorities.

Regular Settlement Monies and securities are exchanged the next business day after the transaction is completed.

Repurchase Agreement (Repos or RPs) a collateralized deposit with a stated maturity, at a financial institution.

Secondary Certificate of Deposit negotiable certificate of deposit, originally issued at least one day prior.

Secondary Market market where previously issued securities are bought and sold.

Securities Portfolio an aggregation of all the different investment securities owned by one investor.

Selling Group group of banks, dealers, etc. whose main responsibility is in selling newly issued securities of a particular obligator.

Settlement Date day agreed upon by the buyer and seller of a security when funds and ownership of securities will be exchanged.

Simple Interest interest earned only on the principal, not including any earned interest.

Skip Settlement Monies and securities are exchanged two business days after the transaction is completed.

State Tax Free not obligated to pay the state taxes on the income received from a security.

Tax Liability obligation by an individual or company to pay a governing body a sum on earnings.

Trade Date the date the transaction is verbally completed between buyer and seller.

Trader a person who maintains a speculative position in securities.

U.S. Treasury Bill a short-term, discounted obligation of the U.S. Government with an initial maturity of one year or less.

U.S. Treasury Bond obligation of the U.S. Government initially issued to mature between ten and thirty years.

U.S. Treasury Note obligation of the U.S. Government initially issued to mature between two and ten years.

Variable Rate Certificates of Deposit certificate of deposit whose assigned coupon rate may fluctuate over the life of the deposit.

When Issued (WI) referred to a security that has been announced for distribution by its issuer, but has not yet been issued. Commonly used as a trading vehicle for large, active trading portfolios.

Yield the percentage rate of return on an investment.

Yield Curve a graph of the relationship between rate of return and the terms to maturities for a security or securities.

Glossary

Yield to Maturity average annual rate of return on an investment if it is held to maturity.

Zero Coupon Bond bonds sold at a deep discount from the face value, that will pay back to the investor the stated face value at maturity.

Appendix G

BIBLIOGRAPHY

Cook, Timothy Q., and Bruce J. Summers (editors). *Instruments of the Money Market*, 5th edition. Federal Reserve Bank of Richmond, 1981.

Fischer, Donald E., and Ronald Jordan. *Security Analysis and Portfolio Management*. Englewood Cliffs, NJ: Prentice-Hall, Inc., 1975.

Handbook of Securities of the United States Government and Federal Agencies and Related Money Market Instruments, 31st edition. New York, NY: First Boston Corporation, 1984.

Kolb, Robert W. *Investments*, 2nd Edition, Glenview, IL: Scott, Foresman and Co., 1989.

Stigum, Marcia. *The Money Market*. Homewood, IL: Dow Jones - Irwin, 1983.

Various Guides and Pamphlets from the Federal Farm Credit Bank, Federal Home Loan Bank, Federal National Mortgage Association and Federal Home Loan Mortgage Corporation, 1989.

ABOUT THE AUTHOR

Jeffrey H. Katz has been employed in the Securities Sales and Trading Department of Union Bank, in Los Angeles, for over eleven years. During this time he has held several sales, trading, and managerial positions, all related to U.S. government and money market securities. Jeff started his career selling U.S. government and money market securities to individuals and small companies that were clients of Union Bank. Next, Jeff traded for, and maintained, the bank's Federal Funds account with the Federal Reserve Bank. Since 1982, Jeff has been involved in selling U.S. government and money market securities to institutional investors. His clients include the traders and portfolio managers of some of the largest municipalities, money funds, pension funds, banks, bank trust departments, corporations, and investment advisors in the country. During this time, Jeff also has managed the institutional sales department. Jeff has been called on to give lectures to bank clients and employees on U.S. government and money market securities. Jeff received his Bachelor of Science in Finance from the University of Illinois in 1979. He earned his Master of Business Administration from Pepperdine University in 1981. Jeff is a NASD Series 7 and MSRB Municipal Bond Representative licensee.

Additional Titles in
The Investor's Self-Teaching Seminars Series
Available from Probus Publishing

Allocating and Managing Your Investment Assets, Richard Koff

Financial Statement Analysis, Charles J. Woelfel

Investing in High-Yield Stocks, Peter D. Heerwagen

Investing in Rental Properties, Robert W. Richards & Grover C. Richards

Trading Stock Index Options, Mikel T. Dodd

Understanding and Managing Investment Risk & Return, David L. Scott

Understanding and Trading Listed Stock Options, Carl F. Luft & Richard K. Sheiner

Understanding and Using Margin, Michael T. Curley

Understanding the Stock Market, David T. Sutton

Using Technical Analysis, Clifford Pistolese

Forthcoming Titles

Calculating, Protecting and Enhancing Your Net Worth, Kevin J. Sears

Understanding and Trading Futures, Carl F. Luft

Your Home as Your Best Investment, Robert W. Richards & Grover C. Richards